THE PRESENCE

Dannie Abse was for many years a chest specialist in a London clinic. A poet, novelist and playwright, he has written and edited more than sixteen books of poetry, as well as books about medicine. He is the author of *Ash on a Young Man's Sleeve* and several autobiographical volumes, the most recent of which, *Goodbye, Twentieth Century*, was published by Pimlico in 2001 to critical acclaim. His most recent novel, *The Strange Case of Dr Simmonds & Dr Glas* was published in 2002 and long-listed for the Booker Prize. In 2003 his *New and Collected Poems* received the Special Commendation of the Poetry Book Society, and *Running Late* received the Roland Mathias Prize in 2007.

ALSO BY DANNIE ABSE

Poetry

Walking Under Water

Tenants of the House

Poems, Golders Green

A Small Desperation

Funland and Other Poems

Collected Poems 1948–1976

Way Out in the Centre

Ask the Bloody Horse

White Coat, Purple Coat: Poems 1948–1988

Remembrance of Crimes Past

On the Evening Road

Arcadia, One Mile

New and Collected Poems

Running Late

Editor

The Hutchinson Book of Post-War British Poets

Twentieth Century Anglo-Welsh Poetry

Voices in the Gallery (with Joan Abse)

The Music Lover's Literary Companion (with Joan Abse)

Plays

The View from Row G: Three plays

Novels

Ash on a Young Man's Sleeve

Some Corner of an English Field

O. Jones, O. Jones

There Was A Young Man from Cardiff

The Strange Case of Dr Simmonds and Dr Glas

Other Prose

Medicine on Trial

A Poet in the Family

A Strong Dose of Myself (Confessions Stories, Essays)

Journals from the Ant Heap

Intermittent Journals

Goodbye, Twentieth Century

The Two Roads Taken

DANNIE ABSE

The Presence

VINTAGE BOOKS
London

Published by Vintage 2008

2 4 6 8 10 9 7 5 3 1

First published in Great Britain in 2007 by
Hutchinson

Vintage
Random House, 20 Vauxhall Bridge Road,
London SW1V 2SA

www.vintage-books.co.uk

Addresses for companies within The Random House Group Limited
can be found at: www.randomhouse.co.uk/offices.htm

The Random House Group Limited Reg. No. 954009

A CIP catalogue record for this book
is available from the British Library

ISBN 9780099531869

The Random House Group Limited supports The Forest Stewardship
Council (FSC), the leading international forest certification
organisation. All our titles that are printed on Greenpeace approved
FSC certified paper carry the FSC logo. Our paper procurement
policy can be found at www.rbooks.co.uk/environment

Printed and bound in Great Britain by
CPI Cox & Wyman, Reading RG1 8EX

For Keren, Susanna and David. Without their encouragement this book would never have been finished. I must also thank Jeremy Robson, Siân Williams, Tony Whittome and Robert Kirby for their warm, sustained and supportive interest. Larne 'Abse' Gogarty, my granddaughter, kindly typed out the manuscript.

D. A.

'... like many people who grieve, I was living in the presence of an invisible being.'

Elaine Pagels

'What really belongs to a man, in life, except what he has already lived?'

Cesare Pavese

The Presence

JOAN ABSE

From the *Guardian*, Saturday June 18th 2005

The writer and art historian Joan Abse, who has died in a traffic accident at the age of seventy-eight, was a woman who managed to marry her political and aesthetic beliefs with both her work and the way she lived her life.

Born Joan Mercer in St Helens, Lancashire, she was educated at the local grammar school. She was politically active early in life, and became branch secretary of the St Helens Independent Labour party at the age of fourteen, the beginning of a long association with that strand of left-of-centre politics closely allied to pacifism and the anti-nuclear movement.

Joan was an early and long-standing member of CND and a supporter of the Greenham Common protesters. Her antipathy to war was unwavering, and in 2003 she participated in the Stop The War march in London.

Evacuated to Cambridge during the Second World War, she completed her education at the London School of Economics under Harold Laski; she met the poet and doctor, Dannie Abse, whom she married in 1951. She worked for several years as a librarian at the *Financial*

Times before the arrival of the children, Keren, Susanna and David. About this time, she and Dannie put down roots in Golders Green, where the family remained.

Besides her family, political and other commitments, Joan enrolled as an adult student at the Courtauld Institute, where she took an MA in art history under Anita Brookner, the foundation for much of her later writing. Her wide-ranging knowledge of art, especially of painting over the past seven centuries, underlay her intelligent and accessible gazetteer, *The Art Galleries Of Britain And Ireland: A Guide To Their Collections* (1975).

That work of reference was supplemented by *Voices In The Gallery* (1986), an anthology of poetry responding to art in the Tate and in other leading galleries, which she co-edited with Dannie. Her interest in the ways in which art forms mesh also produced *The Music Lover's Literary Companion* (1988), again co-edited with Dannie.

Her own publications included *My London School Of Economics* (1977), a volume in a series of anthologies about universities, and *Letters From Wales* (1999), on which I worked with her as publisher. The book was adapted for radio, and it demonstrated her great editorial talent and scholarship.

Joan's outstanding work was *John Ruskin: A Passionate Moralist* (1980), a biography acclaimed on both sides of the Atlantic, and still a key work. Many of Joan's own interests, political, literary and artistic, were central to Ruskin's achievement. His desire to open up the world of art to the common man and progress the debate about art in a social context chimed with his biographer. She

identified with Ruskin's championing of the unfashion-
able (including Turner), his ability to look beyond visual
art into literature and society, and his challenge, by
personal example, to the public and the salon to reap-
praise their taste and their lives.

The biography is an outstanding work of art history
and reading of personality. My copy, a present from
Joan, included a note of typical gentle humour and
modesty: 'You don't have to read the enclosed but, of
course, you will benefit enormously if you do!' I did.

Joan was also an enormous influence on Dannie. Her
perspicacity and intelligent reading of his poetry, fiction,
journals and plays was hugely important; he would
otherwise have been a different writer. Together they
provided each other with a sustaining platform on which
to work; they had shared values.

The aid Joan gave was sometimes very practical.
Dannie liked to tell of his young son, David, entering
his study with a friend. He pointed out a row of books,
all by his father: 'Do you see those books over there?'
asked David. Dannie quickened with pride. 'My Mum
typed all of them.'

Those who knew Joan are unanimous in their
acknowledgement of her kindness, generosity and atten-
tiveness, and of her elegance. She was admired for her
practicality, her commitment to her beliefs, her support
of others, and the way she was at ease with herself. She
was a contemporary woman, engaged, compassionate
and inspiring to so many who met her or read her work.

Her family and all who knew her must reconcile

themselves with the abrupt end to her life – in south Wales, returning from an enjoyable poetry reading. We will do well to look at her loss through her own eyes.

Dannie, who was injured in the accident, and their children survive her.

Mick Felton

Joan Abse, art historian, born September 11th 1926; died June 13th 2005

September 22nd 2005

The past survives however much one tries to drive it down and away from one's consciousness. It rears up provoked by something overheard or a scene, a place, an object, a tune, a scent even. It is inescapable. But I think how I must count my blessings, though it would have been better if Joan not I had been the one who had crawled out of that capsized car. She would have been much more self-sufficient. Count your blessings, son, my mother used to say. A cliché. At times of stress, clichés, family sayings, proverbs, are drawn to the mind like a magnet. I do count my blessings: at night, though I don't sleep well, I am able to lie on my right side now that the stress-fractures of the right thoracic cage have healed; the scar on my chin and neck are hardly visible; my left thumb, though oddly angled, is less troublesome and it is no bad thing that I've lost a stone in weight. Presumably the latter is due as much to my increased metabolic rate as it is to the lack of Joan's tempting and nutritious cooking. At least I hope I haven't developed an over-active thyroid. I take my pulse and note it is raised though not alarmingly so. Do I write all this down as an aide-mémoire for my future self?

I remember a long-ago case history of a woman who suddenly developed a too active thyroid gland. She had been healthy when she began cycling through a long, dark tunnel. A car, with headlights on, cruised slowly behind her, she cycled faster. The car accelerated. She pedalled on, even more frenetically. And still the car followed close to her. When finally she emerged from the tunnel, the car sped past to disappear for ever but her heart-rate had permanently increased, her fingers continued to tremble, and in due course she was diagnosed as suffering from thyrotoxicosis.

Many people enduring a bereavement become physically ill, even prone to develop something sinister. Sir Stanford Cade who took ward rounds when I was a medical student at Westminster Hospital asserted that cancer incidence is greater in individuals enduring emotional imbalance. And experimental studies on rats experiencing stress showed how these animals had less resistance to implanted tumours than those enjoying a more comfortable existence. (Sir Stanford Cade, a radical surgeon of Eastern European origin with a marked guttural accent would often tell his students, 'This ees inoperable. I vill operate.') As long ago as 1960, the Cambridge radiotherapist, J. S. Mitchell, noted how an emotional upheaval following the death of a wife, husband or child caused a recurrence of an apparently healed malignant tumour within a year.

Anyway, I am determined, as much as one consciously can be, not to take the escape route into somatic sickness. Nor am I willing to seek a counsellor though I'm surprised how easily I become lachrymose. Also I can't get over my own timidity – the way I won't easily leave this house for stranger precincts. I hate travelling further than Hampstead, which is only a mile away. I need more than ever the sanctuary of the familiar. I can't even bring myself to visit Cardiff for the day to watch the Bluebirds despite my having a season ticket for the centre stand at Ninian Park. The idea of coming back to Paddington on the train without Joan and then on to an empty, dark house in Golders Green is too daunting. And of course, I've cancelled all my poetry-reading engagements.

Is this anomie I experience when I'm not in familiar surroundings, this territorial timidity, a psychological regression to childhood uncertainties? I was born in Whitchurch Road, Cardiff, but after a year or two we were on the move. To 289 Albany Road, Cardiff. A few years later the wanderlust possessed my parents again and we shifted three minutes away to 237 Albany Road. A few years of stability and doors slamming, and me protesting vainly about moving before we trekked another 500 yards to 66 Albany Road. I hated each move from rented house to house. I didn't realise, as a boy, how much the wanderlust was related to my father's changing financial fortunes.

September 23rd
Letters of consolation — now mainly from abroad — still arrive and touch me to tears. Because of the obituaries in *The Times*, the *Independent*, the *Guardian*, etc. I have received hundreds of letters. One from an artist whom I don't really know but who years ago did a quick portrait of me. I never liked it: I look so melancholy. Now I wonder if the future

haunts all portraits, a preternatural unveiling. It's as if the artist had guessed that one day I would be a man grieving because his dear one had been turned to stone on the M4.

Letters also still come addressed to Joan. I think how my friend, Peter Porter, soon after he lost his wife, Jannice, wrote:

> A card comes to tell you
> you should report
> to have your eyes tested.
>
> But your eyes melted in the fire . . .
> and the only tears, which soon dried,
> fell in the chapel.
>
> Other things still come —
> invoices, subscriptions, renewals,
> Shiny plastic cards promising credit —
> not much for a life spent
> in the service of reality . . .

Apart from those Peter has listed, a plethora of appeals for the many charities subscribed to by Joan drop through the letter box every morning. Joan was so much more a soft touch than I am. Or to put it another way, more generous. But just thinking about Joan turns me over, including writing this. And I say to myself, 'For Chrissake, PULL YOURSELF TOGETHER.'

September 24th
I cry, therefore I am.

September 28th

On Tuesday mornings, for physical and mental health reasons, I've decided to resume attending the Royal Free Hospital club's gym which I have done since the summer of 2001. As has often been my custom, on the way home, I quit the 268 bus at Hampstead to drop into Café Rouge for a light lunch of onion soup, mixed salad and a basket of French bread. Whenever Joan joined me here she would generally choose the tarte which she used to relish. I did not order two glasses of wine. Injurious thoughts.

Soon I became aware of the women on the near next table. I overheard the chatter of French. To hear French spoken in an English French restaurant is somewhat reassuring. But they both spoke so quickly I could not understand the gist of their dialogue. (My French is minimal. In Paris I once ordered some bread and eventually the waiter brought me rabbit.) I gave up attempting to eavesdrop, sipped my onion soup, and found myself thinking of the first time Joan and I visited Paris. We had not booked an hotel and though Joan spoke French adequately we ended up sleeping in a Montmartre brothel.

Then

It was the late 1940s. I was an impoverished medical student walking the wards at Westminster Hospital and Joan had recently graduated from the LSE to find library work at the *Financial Times*. Not yet married we lived in a single but spacious bedsitting room at 50 Belsize Square, Swiss Cottage. When I earned £15, a generous fee for writing an article for *World Review*, I suggested we could spend some summer days in Paris.

At a Montparnasse café made notorious by being favoured by such existentialist figures as Jean-Paul Sartre we encountered Irwin, an American, a rich American, whom we knew when he sojourned earlier that year at Swiss Cottage. Already, then, he had tried to enlist some of our friends to join his commune, geographically far from Europe. He was confident that the Cold War would inevitably lead to an atomic conflagration that would engulf us all. He had bought an old seafaring boat and he had begun to hire a crew. His plans, he assured us in that Paris café, were far advanced and desperately he urged us to choose to be saved.

'Make up your mind. It's a Kierkegaard either/or situation.' I had read little of the Danish philosopher but dropping his name was appropriate in that existentialist café. In his texts about choice I was aware Kierkegaard had cited the fairy-tale parable where mermaids enticed human victims into their sea caves and into their power by playing demonic music. To break free from their enslavement the victims had to play the same music backwards – a task impossible for most to perform. In short and to simplify: choice = destiny, QED.

'It's time,' agreed Irwin. 'You will come with us. There'll be no turning back.'

The Garden of Eden destination Irwin had selected for his commune lay far away from it all in the mid-Pacific: Bikini Island. Returned to Swiss Cottage we learnt months later that Irwin's old boat had sunk in the Thames

estuary. It was just as well: in May 1951 the Americans
tested the first H-bomb on the Bikini atoll.

We never ran into Irwin again. I imagine him
dreaming of a different safe haven, reciting not
Kierkegaard but Gerard Manley Hopkins:

> I have decided to go
>   Where springs not fail,
> To fields where flies no sharp and sided hail
>   And a few lilies blow.
>
> And I have asked to be
>   Where no storms come,
> Where the green swell is in the havens dumb,
>   And out of the swing of the sea.

October 10th

A writer's block: a bee against a windowpane.

One can't accept the gift of solitude if one feels
lonely. Now I understand what Dr Johnson meant when
he told his Mrs Thrale, 'Grief is a species of idleness.'

October 14th

I'm told diary keeping can be therapeutic. Certainly
it is a prescription for the diarist to prove to himself
that he is alive. Like a prisoner's graffiti on a cell wall,
surely the words imply, 'I am here, I exist.' Moreover,
should the diarist feel, as I do now, a filtering loss of
interest in the loud streets outside and own the griever's
inability – as Freud put it – 'to adopt any possible
new object of love', then just writing this and that

may bring me out into the world as well as into myself.

Since the accident on June 13th I've written little. Without work the days seem purposeless and Joan is nowhere and no white freesias will ever again grace this house in Golders Green. Now, though, the proofs of *Running Late* have arrived. Hutchinson intend to publish this new book of poems next spring.

Having reread the poems, the sweet and the harsh, I think it needs an introductory poem. I've always assented to Louis Pasteur's dictum, 'chance favours the prepared mind'. My mind is prepared to write such a poem so I await the three strange angels. Admit them!

Then

In 1994 I wrote such an introductory poem for *On the Evening Road*. It addressed (anonymously) Joan who was always my most sympathetic and shrewd reader. I called the poem 'Proposal'. Now I walk the indigo road alone but may I, with luck, still find an eagle's feather for *Running Late*.

Proposal

Herschel, thrilled, observed a new star
and named it to honour a King;

Dr Livingstone found for his Queen
a waterfall, 'smoke which sounded';

and tactful Corot gave Daumier
a house 'to upset the landlord'.

What dare I promise? Mountain signposts
are few and treasures I have none.

Yet come with me, congenial, far,
up the higher indigo roads.

There, memory is imagination
and we may find an eagle's feather.

October 16th

Ania, my brother Leo's wife, phoned to ask me to drive
Reva Berstock — an old friend of the Abse family —
from Hampstead where she lives to their house in
Chiswick for Sunday lunch.

All through the journey on the North Circular
Road, I felt anxious for I have driven no distance at
all since the accident on June 13th. I drove slowly, as
if I were an L driver, one, moreover, absurdly concerned
that some lethal car would again crash into me from
behind.

I do not know whether Reva was oblivious of my
nervousness. She just talked away in her pleasant Irish
accent affirming how she no longer works as a child
psychiatrist at the Tavistock Clinic. Retired she may be,
but Reva knows better than most that in our natures
we belong half to the cultivated garden and half to the
dark forest. Later, she asked me how I was coping, and
I confessed, perhaps melodramatically, that for intermittent hours each day I feel like an exile in the Land
of Desolation.

Then

At one of Reva's dinner parties I was engaged in conversation when Reva ushered in another guest and said, 'Dannie, here, used to be good at cricket.' I looked up at the smiling new guest. 'I was a crackhand,' I swanked. 'Captain of the school cricket team, you know!'

'Let me introduce you. This is Mike Brearley,' Reva said triumphantly. Perhaps some of the guests did not know Brearley had been Captain of England because no one laughed. Trying to recover, I told Mike Brearley how years ago a girlfriend of mine had once said that I was a very good bowler because I hit the bat every time.

October 20th

I was waiting for the 268 bus outside Waterstones in Hampstead when one man in the queue began talking to himself. At one point he seemed to be addressing me. I smiled appeasingly. A mistake. On the 268 bus he deliberately sat next to me – he smelt of a wet mackintosh – and began to whistle.

At Jack Straw's Castle he addressed me again but I couldn't make out what he was saying. Soon he resumed whistling. When, at Golders Green, I swiftly left the bus so did he. I had the feeling that I was being followed. Not so. I looked over my shoulder several times before I reached lamplit Hodford Road. Well, even private detectives sometimes imagine they are being followed.

October 21st

A spider in my morning bath. We all experience minor triumphs such as when we consciously avoid stepping on an ant or when we refrain from swatting a fly. Then for a few seconds, a few seconds only, we may experience the euphoria of the gods.

To pray, though, to the gods, or to the God — what arrogance! It is like addressing the vast sky behind the stars and saying, 'Here *I* am.' Reversed thunder, indeed! as George Herbert indicated, along with other definitions of prayer:

Prayer

Prayer, the Church's banquet, Angel's age,
    God's breath in man returning to his birth,
    The soul in paraphrase, heart in pilgrimage,
The Christian plummet sounding heaven and earth;

Engine against th' Almighty, sinner's tower,
    Reversed thunder, Christ-side-piercing spear,
    The six days' world-transposing in an hour,
A kind of tune, which all things hear and fear;

Softness, and peace, and joy, and love, and bliss,
    Exalted Manna, gladness of the best,
    Heaven in ordinary, men well drest,
The Milky Way, the bird of Paradise,

    Church-bells beyond the stars heard, the soul's blood,
    The land of spices, something understood.

Then

When I was a child like the early kabbalists I asked, 'What's the essence of Creation? From whence have we come?' Actually I asked, 'Mama who made the world?' 'God,' she answered. My mother, unlike my father, was a Believer. Friday night, the beginning of the Jewish Sabbath, she would light two candles, place her hands over her eyes and mutter a prayer which concluded, 'Let there be peace in the world.'

What I was led to believe was that the Author of mankind and of all life could intervene on one's behalf, especially with the help of my prayer and my being 'a good boy'. There are portraits whose eyes follow one about the room. God, surely, had those kind of mobile eyes! Dylan Thomas's cousin had put it well: 'Thou canst see everything, right down deep in our hearts; Thou canst see us when the sun has gone; Thou canst see us when there aren't any stars, in the gravy blackness, in the deep, deep, deep, deep pit . . . in the terrible shadows, pitch black, pitch black; Thou canst see everything we do . . . O, God, mun, you're like a bloody cat!'

When I was a child I thought as a child and believed that God could read even my secret thoughts, my velleities. Later, as an adolescent, I happened on Llewellyn Powys's *The Pathetic Fallacy* in which he argues that religion sprang out of fear. I agreed. I became agnostic and certainly knew that if God existed he could not be shut within the confines of synagogue, chapel, church, or mosque with all their crazy prescriptions, their regulated liturgies and rites and dead schedules. Later still, on rare occasions, when I have, as it were, fallen through a hole in the air into wonder I have been persuaded that, as Thomas Aquinas wrote, 'The truths of revelations are not the same as the truths of reason.' But I have used these experiences not in the moral realm but in an attempt to write poems while sitting comfortably in my study far from the thistle-eating donkey and the desert of religion.

October 23rd

How sorry should we feel for a man's lonely sobriety when everybody else in the room is drunk?

Despair now is this side of the fence.

October 28th

I have returned the corrected proofs of *Running Late* to Tony Whittome along with an introductory poem which I've called 'Summoned'. I hope it's OK. Usually I wait months for the rosy lenses to clear before sending out a poem for publication. I've dedicated the book: *To Joan Abse who was killed in a car crash, June 13th, 2005.* Just writing that dedication here unsettles the too prompt tearducts of my eyes. Perhaps it would be better not to mention the car crash. I can imagine how the dedication may appear to a sour critical eye: that I have too overt designs to gain sympathy from the reader. So perhaps I should simply dedicate the book: *To Joan.* Or: *In memory of Joan Abse 1926–2005.*

I'll be advised by Tony.

I wonder if *Running Late* will be my last book of poems? Yeats and Hardy, in their old age, had a wonderful efflorescence of their inspiration and talent. I cannot claim that, but I'm not displeased with the poems in *Running Late*. Am I deluded? Freud in his paper 'Mourning and Melancholia' remarks how in mourning, unlike in melancholia, there is no loss of self-esteem!

Anyway, now that the proofs have been returned, in order to avoid the further negative sloth of my last four and a half months since Joan's death, I've decided to continue this diary/journal/anthology. I don't perceive more poems on the horizon or another novel or play. But to write, simply to write (which is something I've done ever since my teenage years) may become an antidote to my widower's depression.

Then

I had been deluded about my first book of poems, *After Every Green Thing*. (I had taken the title from the book of Job – the ass who searches after every green thing. I had followed the Job example of Alun Lewis whose last book of poetry was *Ha! Ha! Among the Trumpets*.) Hutchinson had published my book in 1948 when I was still a medical student at Westminster Hospital. One patient I had become friendly with happened to be a publisher's rep. It was he who suggested I send my neophyte manuscript to Hutchinson. When it appeared I thought my first slim volume to be terrific! Several years had to pass before I perceived the many defects in *After Every Green Thing*. I had been intoxicated by words, by the polyphony of words, and my use of them had been too arbitrary and too naïve.

I had actually submitted *After Every Green Thing* to Hutchinson in 1945 and six months or so later I received a letter from a Mrs Webb. She invited me to her office in Princes Gate. There she showed me two readers' reports. One reader bristled with indignation and rubbished my poems; the other wildly suggested I was a young genius.

Mrs Webb decided to send the manuscript to a third reader, to a Professor Wilfred Childe at the University of Leeds. He must have been in kindly but premature senescence for he recommended that *After Every Green Thing* should be published. So two years later my embarrassing first volume of verse was published. I was given an advance of £50 on account of royalties and when the book appeared it so happened that Walter Hutchinson, the chairman of the company, committed suicide.

October 30th

When I read the morning newspaper with its continual bloody news about Iraq where they are pissing on the dead, I often think of Harold Wilson and how he sensibly managed to keep us out of the Vietnam War. Blair must have a dangerous combative nature, though he always seems too placatory when challenged. Observe his half puzzled smile, 'Look . . . I . . .' He was disastrously placatory when it came to confronting Bush, who in his presidency is by murder fed, and by murder clothed. All those capital letter speeches of his:

DEMOCRACY. FREEDOM. There should be a poster in the White House and at 10 Downing Street of Alex Comfort's poem, 'Notes For My Son'. It should be there permanently whoever happens to occupy these civilised but savage citadels.

Notes For My Son

Remember when you hear them beginning to say
    Freedom
Look carefully — see who it is that they want you to
    butcher.

Remember, when you say that the old trick would
    not have fooled you for a moment
That every time it is the trick which seems new.

Remember that you will have to put in irons
Your better nature, if it will desert to them.

Remember, remember their faces — watch them
    carefully:
For every step you take is on somebody's body,

And every cherry you plant for them is a gibbet
And every furrow you turn for them is a grave.

Remember, the smell of burning will not sicken you
If they persuade you that it will thaw the world.

Beware. The blood of a child does not smell so bitter
If you have shed it with a high moral purpose.

So that because the woodcutter disobeyed
They will not burn her today or any day.

So that for lack of a joiner's obedience
The crucifixion will now not take place.

So that when they come to sell you their bloody
   corruption
you will gather the spit of your chest
and plant it in their faces.

Then

I am in the Westminster Hospital Medical School's
student union. It is 1947 and instead of attending a
ward round I am writing a poem called 'Letter to
Alex Comfort'. Alex, at that time, was considered to
be one of the few important poets to have emerged
in England since the beginning of the Second World
War. He would also soon become appreciated as a
leading gerontologist studying and researching the
ageing process.

I knew Alex Comfort a little during the early post-
war years. We had much in common. He was only a
few years older than me. He, a young doctor; I a young
medical student. We both wrote poetry and I warmed
to his doctrine of disobedience.

Perhaps Alex was somewhat too interested in accu-
mulating money. Long before he left London for
California where he had been invited to be a Fellow at
the Institute for Higher Studies in Santa Barbara, he
said to me, 'We should try and write lyrics for pop

songs. That's where the cash is.' Even so, I was surprised when decades later he became renowned as the author of a hot-selling graphic book about sex. His poetry reputation, alas, did not outlast its season.

But gerontology held his perdurable interest. In his London days he already realised how old people become less visible and he felt a deep compassion for them. Socrates called the old, 'pessimistic, malicious, distrustful, suspicious and small-minded – attributes that would suit them for politics'. I'm not sure how Alex would have responded to that.

He knew, of course, medical history – of the long-held conception that longevity and sexuality were linked. When Brown Séquard injected himself with testicular extracts, when Steinach tried to stimulate growth of the testicular cells by increasing their blood supply, when Voronoff transplanted chimpanzee testicles into a patient, these early modern gerontologists were only acting out the fundamental age equation that sexual vigour equalled longevity. It's not as simple as that: eunuchs live as long as the rest of us, if not longer.

Alex himself did not know advanced old age. He was no eunuch.

October 31st

To avoid self-pity and insistent glooms I need corposant distractions apart from this diary. Other pursuits, equally inconsequential, consist of playing chess with Peter Gutmann or Paul Harrison or Tony Whittome, watching football or slouching before the TV set. Over the weekend I roused myself to begin reading the post-humously published *Party in the Blitz* by Elias Canetti. What I've read so far indicates it is an unfinished draft-extension of Canetti's earlier Nobel Prize-winning autobiographical volumes. But the portraits he presents are distorted as if seen through a convex mirror. And Canetti comes through as an unpleasant snob, one too pleased to keep company with Lady This and the Duke of That.

I was unaware of his class snobbery when I frequently sat at his table in the Cosmo Coffee House in Swiss Cottage during the 1950s. I was intellectually enriched by doing so, and I continue to be grateful for his long ago concern for my youthful welfare and for his curiosity about my youthful work. It was through Canetti that an early play of mine was performed at the ICA, and several 'existential' poems I wrote were provoked by our café dialogues, or through books he had introduced me to. *Specimens of Bushman Folklore* by the anthropologists Bleek and Lloyd was but one text he lent me that I found seminal. 'One of the glories of world literature', asserts Canetti in *Party in the Blitz*. A particular legend from that book haunts me still. It concerns a young hunter asleep at noon who is discovered by a lion. The hunter feigns to be dead and the lion, puzzled, licks tears from the young man's eyes. Later the hunter escapes; but afterwards the lion seeks no other prey than 'the young man whose tears he had drunk'.

Decades after I read that Bushmen legend (see Appendix One) I watched a David Attenborough TV documentary which focused on a lion amidst a herd of antelopes. When it selected one particular antelope to hunt and to bloodily strike the other antelopes sensed they were safe and continued grazing calmly. Could a lion's singularity of purpose in choosing a particular victim have inspired the Bushman legend, I wonder?

November 1st

The way Canetti writes about Iris Murdoch: 'she had not one serious thought'; 'the facile plausibility of her books'; 'you could call Iris Murdoch the bubbling Oxford stewpot'; 'everything I despise about English life is in her', suggests that Canetti must have been an *ashamed* ex-lover of hers and one who had been truly defeated, profoundly wounded.

Then

I was unused to Canetti praising living authors. His literary heroes were safely dead: Stendhal, Kafka, Musil, etc. So when Canetti told me in 1953 that he had discovered a new young novelist, Iris Murdoch, I looked forward to reading her book, *Under the Net*. Canetti had asserted it to be 'a remarkable work. It's not a one-off by the way. She has an earlier volume in the drawer.' He, secretive as always, did not tell me that he had begun an affair with Iris Murdoch.

When *Under the Net* appeared I enjoyed reading it, but it was not Stendhal, not Kafka, not Musil. I think it was then that I first questioned Canetti's austere, bruising value judgements. When I asked him when he was going to complete his work-in-progress, *Crowds and Power*, he said, 'I'm not going to make the mistake of Freud – publish too quickly and then have to contradict myself.' And he brilliantly ventilated his reservations also about the work of Eliot and Graham Greene.

His literary fastidiousness could, on occasions, be absurd, even comical. When he had seen me in company with the novelist, Wolf Mankowitz, he advised me, 'You shouldn't have anything to do with that fellow. He'll pollute you. Do you know he writes a column on diet for the *Evening Standard*?' And when I carried a slim volume, *Word Over All* by C. Day Lewis into the Cosmo and expressed my pleasure in the book, he said with disdain, 'Dannie, Day Lewis writes detective stories. He's not a serious poet.'

November 2nd
Lunch at the Café Rouge in Hampstead with the young Welsh poet, Owen Sheers. His new book, *Skirrid Hill*, is much better than the original manuscript which Seren Books sent me to comment on a year or so ago.

Over lunch we discuss 'voice' in poetry, the importance of it to be recognisably singular. I heard myself say, 'Repetition makes a style.' (Owen Sheers's *Skirrid Hill* owns a variousness of subject matter.) 'Yes,' Owen agreed, 'but one can only repeat theme not style.' He was right, of course. Style is an unconscious attribute. Poetry is written in the brain but the brain is bathed in blood. Its intoxicating effects are dependent on unconscious engenderings and proliferations. So a writer wondering whether he is gifted with an individual style confronts a dilemma. He looks at a mirror but sees no one there. Others, though, can see the reflection well enough.

At best a writer can come to be familiar only with his stylistic mannerisms. And when he does apprehend these he should deliberately eschew them. Graham Greene was but one who recognised his own mannerisms. Years ago he entered a *New Statesman* competition: 'Write in the manner of Graham Greene'. Interestingly, the anonymous winner of the second prize turned out to be Graham Greene!

Owen Sheers, apart from being genuinely talented, is a very agreeable young person. Perhaps he will be damned to be famous one day for, like so many of 'my colleagues in the art' who have to make a living as freelance writers, he is not afraid of publicity. I've often thought of poetry as a vocation, even a destiny, rather than a career but sometimes I wish that on certain occasions in my life I had not retreated from the limelight. Perhaps, I was too arrogant to step into it. Pasternak's 'It is not seemly', translated by his sister, comes to mind; it is a poem I treasure, one of many that inhabit my life in sense and in sound.

It is not seemly

It is not seemly to be famous:
Celebrity does not exalt;
There is no need to hoard your writings
And to preserve them in a vault.

To give your all — this is creation,
And not to deafen and eclipse.
How shameful, when you have no meaning,
To be on everybody's lips!

Try not to live as a pretender,
But so to manage your affairs
That you are loved by wide expanses,
And hear the call of future years.

Leave blanks in life, not in your papers,
And do not ever hesitate
To pencil out whole chunks, whole chapters
Of your existence, of your fate.

Into obscurity retiring
Try your development to hide,
As autumn mist on early mornings
Conceals the dreaming countryside.

Another, step by step, will follow
The living imprint of your feet;
But you yourself must not distinguish
Your victory from your defeat.

And never for a single moment
Betray your credo or pretend,
But be alive — this only matters —
Alive and burning to the end.

November 4th

Just after 7 p.m. Jeremy Robson calls. Dine together? His wife, Carole, is away in France for a few days. So we trek around the corner from our houses to Sam's, the local brashly lit fish and chip shop. Jeremy tells me how one of his authors, Maureen Lipman, mourns for her husband, Jack Rosenthal. 'She makes herself frantically busy, acting and singing strenuously in a play in the West End, writing a column for the *Guardian*, rushing here, doing that, speaking at charity functions, etc.' Jeremy knows that since the accident, for the most part I rarely venture further than Hampstead and am now too inactive. At present, often, I sit and do not even stare. I tell Jeremy about my Uncle Isidore who when asked, 'What do you do?' replied truthfully, 'Nothing. And I don't do that until after lunch.'

Then

Several authors published by Robson Books happen to be showbiz people. Once at a Robson dinner party, Uri Geller was the guest of honour, his book having recently been published. When Joan and I arrived he was giving his considerable full-front attention to the splendidly glamorous Abigail who wore an eye-diverting low-cut dress. Jeremy introduced me, adding helpfully, 'Dannie's a poet.' Geller glanced at me, then turned to Abigail saying, '*I* write poetry!' Then he continued to tell us all about his early background and how he had come to realise he had a magical gift.

He demanded to be the general centre of rapt attention until Michael Bentine, a one-time Goon arrived. Soon it was Bentine who embeamed the room. He asserted that by staring at clouds he could disperse them. 'I have to concentrate,' he insisted. He had learnt his magic, he affirmed, in Peru, and his own profound belief in the supernatural had allowed supernatural incidents to occur frequently. At last Uri Geller, latterly ignored, competitively asked, somewhat plaintively I thought, 'Would you like me to bend some spoons for you?'

'Oh yes,' said Abigail putting the palms of her hands together as if in prayer.

After the spoon and knife bending, Geller even stimulated Abigail's broken watch to tick again. Or so Abigail said. I reckon the result was Geller 2, Bentine 2.

November 5th

Keren visited me, 'Dad I have some bad news . . . Wilfred died last night.'

The last time I telephoned my dear brother at his home in Charlottesville, Virginia, I guessed that he was dying. He had been ill for a long time and had lost his old merriment. He could hardly talk. 'I'm hanging in there,' he gasped. Wilfred hung in there until our father's birthday, November 4th.

Apart from Joan I owe more to my eldest brother than to any other person. Such debts! Through Wilfred I became a doctor, inheriting his medical textbooks all of which, by the way, had an inscription on the fly leaf — *nil desperandum*. He encouraged me in my literary pursuits, never finding fault even with my sixth-form schoolboy attempts. He would read my books, come to my poetry readings, attend my plays and, invariably, would give me an enthusiastic generous response.

I weep for Wilfred. Yet it is hard to mourn for more than one person at a time.

Then

The end of summer schoolterm at St Illtyd's, Cardiff. I hear a car's hooter signal three times outside. Then, after a pause, three more punctual raspberries. I put up my hand. 'Please Brother Vincent may I be excused?' He, of course, expects my absence to be temporary. But Tacitus can wait. I do not return to the classroom for I am joining Wilfred in his newly bought red MG. My bathing costume is wrapped up in a towel on the back seat. I'm released. I'm free. I'm mitching. My big brother is driving me on the A48 to the village of Ogmore-by-Sea, which is halfway between Swansea and Cardiff, on the coast of course. Facing across the cutlery-glinting sea are the small hills of Somerset which are some fifteen miles away. There the man from Porlock lives. Soon I'll be swimming in the grey, twitching conger-eel Bristol Channel. Meanwhile it's only a matter of time before Wilfred hums his favourite Robbie Burns song about the unfaithfulness of a lover.

The Banks o' Doon

Ye flowery banks o' bonnie Doon,
How can ye blume sae fair!
How can ye chant, ye little birds,
An I sae fu' o' care!

Thou'll break my heart, thou bonnie bird,
That sings upon the bough;
Thou minds me o' the happy days
When my fause luve was true.

Thou'll break my heart, thou bonnie bird,
That sings beside thy mate;
For sae I sat, and sae I sang,
And wist na o' my fate.

Aft hae I rov'd by bonnie Doon,
To see the woodbine twine;
And ilka bird sang o' its luve;
And sae did I o' mine.

Wi' lightsome heart I pu'd a rose,
Frae aff its thorny tree;
And my fause luver staw the rose,
But left the thorn wi' me.

November 6th
Dissatisfied with myself. Must try and write something,
though I know the most wise and the most stupid say
nothing. Oh the dignity of saying nothing!

Across the other side of Hodford Road, the gold of
west-facing windows.

November 16th

Wilfred's youngest son, Nathan, who is based in Washington where he works as a journalist, intends to come over for Joan's memorial at Lauderdale House in Highgate.

When I phoned my brother's house in Charlottesville Nathan was often in caring attendance and it was Nathan who reported to me the true state of Wilfred's health. Elizabeth, understandably, was more reluctant to dwell on unhappy detail and she continued, until his terminal days, to be optimistic. Or so it seemed.

Then

When Nathan was no higher than the desk I'm now seated at, he and his parents visited us one summer while we stayed at our house 'Green Hollows' in Ogmore. They arrived late in the evening. For a small boy he had a curiously low, gravelly American voice: 'Hey, guys, do you have any pistachio ice cream round here?'

Ogmore-by-Sea had closed down for the night: the post office and the other two shops were shut and the queue of lamp posts emphasised the emptiness of the coast road. Out at sea, beyond the invisible Tusker Rock, the lighthouses spawned at intervals their bright exclamation marks and across the slate-black Bay, towards the lion's paw of Porthcawl's promontory, the dazzle of the fake jewel illuminations of Porthcawl's fair attracted Nathan's attention. When told of the fair's delights: the figure of 8, the merry-go-round, the dodgy dodgems, the slow speedboats, the thinnest fat lady, the smallest Patagonian giant, Nathan growled, 'It's dead round here, man. Let's go over there to civilisation.'

The next day, my American diminutive nephew disappeared. Wilfred and Elizabeth did not seem to be disconcerted. 'He often wanders off on his own.' We did not see him until late in Ogmore's slow-paced sundown.

Nathan had tried to walk to Porthcawl. He had strolled past the bungalows to the beach, crossed the river (the tide was out), walked below the tall sand dunes (the second highest in Europe), circumvented Happy Valley with its unhappy accumulation of caravans, past Newton until, over-tired, recreant, he attempted to phone us so that we could pick him up in the car. But in the public phone booth he bungled the call, using up what British coins he had. He managed, though, to contact the operator. He explained his predicament and suggested the charges for his phone call could be reversed.

'He was one damn fool,' husky-voiced Nathan continued, 'I told him how old I was but the guy said, "stop puttin' on that stupid fake American accent," then he cut me off.'

November 19th

There must have been more than a hundred people at Lauderdale House — relatives and friends. Some had come from the USA, some from Italy. Others from Scotland and of course a number from Wales. Many were literary people — many poets as well as other writers: Arnold Wesker, Ann Thwaite, Michael Holroyd, Patrick Hannan, Derwent May, Margaret Drabble, etc.

As Jeremy Robson said in his speech, 'Joan would have been amazed to see so many people here tonight . . . such was her true modesty.'

My son-in-law, Paul Gogarty, acted as MC, first introducing David. 'I still hear my mother's voice,' my son confessed. 'I can still hear her advice. Her voice in my head is the same, sensible, loving part of me. The more kind, tolerant part. I miss my mother.'

After further touching speeches from Cary Archard who spoke of Joan's literary gifts and Pat Wain of her love of painting and her wide knowledge as an art historian, my daughters read extracts from Joan's writings. Then there were poems. Tony Curtis concluded by reading my somewhat wry 'Thankyou Note'.

Thankyou Note

for the unbidden swish of morning curtains
you opened wide – letting sleep-baiting shafts
of sunlight enter to lie down by my side;
for adagio afternoons when you did the punting
(my toiling eyes researched the shifting miles of sky);
for back-garden evenings when you chopped the wood
and I, incomparably, did the grunting;
(a man too good for this world of snarling
is no good for his wife – truth's the safest lie);

for applauding my poetry, O most perceptive spouse;
for the improbable and lunatic, my darling;
for amorous amnesties after rancorous rows
like the sweet-nothing whisperings of a leafy park

after the blatant noise of a city street
(exit booming cannons, enter peaceful ploughs);
for kindnesses the blind side of my night-moods;
for lamps you brought in to devour the dark.

Later that night, alone, I thought how profoundly my
offspring lament the death of their mother; and I recalled
my own grief when my parents died – my father in 1964,
and my mother in 1981. Yet my grieving was soon attenuated – I had an independent life. Thankfully so do
Keren, Susanna and David. But I have been so dependent
on Joan. Absolutely. Mentally, emotionally, physically.

November 30th
I procrastinated. To go or not to go to the launch of
the Poetry Archive at the British Library. I had read the
list of poets who had been recorded and doubtless many
of them would be there. Because the literary world is a
small one many would know about the accident through
gossip or would have read the obituaries for Joan in
June. A number had attended Joan's memorial – Anthony
Thwaite, Fleur Adcock, William Oxley, Elaine Feinstein,
Peter Porter, Alan Brownjohn, John Fuller among them.
Other acquaintances such as Seamus Heaney, George
Szirtes, Ruth Padel, Hugo Williams and Roger McGough
might passively stumble out consoling words – it's the
thing to do – and touch me into lachrymose embar-
rassment. I did go finally and some of them did.

I was particularly glad to meet Carol Hughes again. I
had not seen her since the memorial for Ted at Westminster

Abbey. We spoke of that time in 1971 when she and Ted joined the other British Council poets selected to tour Israel. Carol and Ted were more or less on their honeymoon. During the week I would often see the newly married couple hand in hand as if posing for a happy wedding photograph. And in Nazareth, at the Basilica of the Annunciation, when Ted Hughes put his arm around Carol's waist we were all startled because the Christian Arab guide shouted angrily, 'This is no place for love!'

As we stood there in the library I reminded Carol of this and that and especially how, one afternoon, I spirited her away so that she could help me choose a decorated garment as a present for Joan from the Arab bazaar stalls in Old Jerusalem. She proved to be an expert haggler.

Then

In a Haifa theatre, Ted Hughes, D. J. Enright, Jeremy Robson, Peter Porter and myself were again on stage after performances in Tel Aviv and Jerusalem. The chairman who introduced us was irritatingly formal like one observing the etiquette of a cemetery. When Ted Hughes read from his new book *Crow* the audience, to my surprise, occasionally laughed. I found nothing funny in Ted's Crow poems which seemed to me to have been written from his usual luminous centre on a black tangent over a black chasm. I wanted to hush the audience. They were Jewish. I was Jewish. Ridiculously I felt responsible for their behaviour! Afterwards, though, they applauded Ted fulsomely. Well, as the Swiss say, 'a good audience also creates'.

Later in conversation with Ted I realised he had been

pleased that his poems needled the audience into laughter. Apparently he'd intended his Crow poems to be edged with black humour. Even so, poems such as 'How Water Began to Play' hardly made me smile. Indeed, that particular piece induced a poignant profound seriousness in me each time Ted softly, ferociously, read it.

How Water Began to Play

Water wanted to live
It went to the sun it came weeping back
Water wanted to live
It went to the trees they burned it came weeping back
They rotted it came weeping back
Water wanted to live
It went to the flowers they crumpled it came weeping back
It wanted to live
It went to the womb it met blood
It came weeping back
It went to the womb it met knife
It came weeping back
It went to the womb it met maggot and rottenness
It came weeping back it wanted to die

It went to time it went through the stone door
It came weeping back
It went searching through all space for nothingness
It came weeping back it wanted to die

Till it had no weeping left

It lay at the bottom of all things
Utterly worn out   utterly clear

December 3rd

I like Milein Cosman as I did her late husband, Hans Keller. When Milein responds to a poem, to a piece of music, to a painting, or to a person, she does so with bubbling enthusiasm. 'Tremendous,' she says with relish, almost jumping in the air in the same way she used to do some fifty years ago.

At her home in Hampstead I spoke of her portraits of musicians which, at present, enliven the restaurant wall at the Wigmore Hall. I did not know she also had a portfolio of poet-portraits though, some years ago, she had drawn John Fuller and myself playing chess. When she showed me her study of T. S. Eliot I asked her whether she had ever drawn Sidney Keyes who I knew had been in unrequited love with her when he was a student at Oxford. I remembered how his contemporary, Philip Larkin, had described Keyes's eyes as 'disturbing'.

'Yes, I did draw Sidney – but I never managed to do a good one,' Milein said.

Few people read Sidney Keyes's poems now though he was one of the most *promising* poets of the twentieth century – one who, had he not been killed in Tunisia in 1942 aged only twenty, would surely have matured to have become valued as much as, say, Philip Larkin. The best of his youthful elegiac verses of love and death can still intrigue readers who are ready to forgive the occasional stage props of florid romanticism.

'He loved visiting churchyards,' Milein said. 'On

our first walk together he took me to one in Longwall. I liked Sidney and admired him but . . . It's hard to be unable to respond to another's deep feelings.'

I thought of Keyes's love poems – some dedicated to Milein. The one I like best is his cadenced 'Hopes for a Lover' which I know more or less by heart.

Hopes for a Lover

I'd have you proud as red brocade
And such a sight as Venus made
Extravagantly stepping from a shell.

I'd have you clear your way before
With such a look as Aias wore
On his way back from hell.

I'd have you strong as spider's strand
And all volcanic as the land
Where the nymph fooled that cunning Ulysses.

I'd have you arrogantly ride
Love's flurry, as the turning seas
Bore Arion upon a fish.
My last and dearest wish—
That you should let the arrows of my pride
Come at you again and again and never touch you.

Then

The first time I saw Milein Cosman was when we both happened to exit from Zwemmer's bookshop in the Charing Cross Road. Must have been 1946 or 1947. I thought, what a beautiful girl, and decided to follow her. Almost immediately she was met and embraced by a smiling young man and they went off together arm in arm. I recall staring blankly at the window of Zwemmer's bookshop for almost a minute . . .

December 6th

As usual this morning, I woke up much too early. About 5 a.m. They say that such oneiric mornings are a sign of clinical depression. Certainly, as I lie in the darkness of the curtained bedroom, I often think of Joan only to discover I am crying. I was doing so this pre-dawn morning when shockingly the telephone sounded. Startled, I reached out to pick up the damn thing to query, 'Hello?' Nothing, no one. For a moment, one adrenal moment, irrationally I felt as if Joan was trying to get through to me. The last few months I've woken up a few times imagining an hallucinatory voice calling me softly, intimately, 'Dannie'.

Freud in his lecture 'The Poet and Daydreaming' speaks of how every musing fancy contains the fulfilment of a wish. So it was for me soon after the accident in June when I fantasised that Joan had not been killed but was merely staying away with friends. That fantasy led me to write perhaps too quickly a love poem – 'Postcard to His Wife'

Postcard to His Wife

Wish you were here. It's a calm summer's day
and the dulcamara of memory
is not enough. I confess without you
I know the impoverishment of self
and the Venus de Milo is only stone.

So come home. The bed's too big! Make excuses.
Hint we are agents in an obscure drama
and must go North to climb 2000 feet
up the cliffs of Craig y Llyn to read
some cryptic message on the face of a rock.

Anything! But come home. Then we'll motor,
just you, just me, through the dominion
of Silurian cornfields, follow the whim
of twisting narrow lanes where hedges
have wild business with roses and clematis.

Or we could saunter to the hunkered blonde
sand dunes and, blessed, mimic the old gods
who enacted the happy way to be holy.
Meanwhile, dear, your husband is so uxorious
absence can't make Abse's heart grow fonder.

December 8th
Overheard in the local Sainsbury's while I was shopping: 'OK I may not know what I'm talking about
but anybody with a bit of sense would agree with
me.'

December 9th

This morning, shaving in the bathroom, I thought how aged I look. The young sometimes make gargoyle faces in the mirror. The old don't have to! I've lost a stone in weight since the accident and I begin more and more to resemble my lean father in his later years. My mother enjoyed reiterating, 'When I was young, everybody in Ystalyfera and our Swansea Valley used to refer to your father and me as The Beauty and The Beast.'

Richard Ellmann related a story much loved by James Joyce about an old man who early in the twentieth century lived in the Blasket Islands and who had never visited the nearby south-west coast of Ireland. He did so eventually and, at a bazaar, picked up a small hand mirror, something he had never seen before. He stared at it with wonder. 'Father!' he exclaimed. He took the small looking-glass back to the Blaskets. Every now and then he stopped rowing to take the mirror out of his pocket, gazed into it and said happily, 'Father, Father.'

Back in the Blaskets he kept his new treasured possession in his pocket and would not show it to his wife. She became suspicious. Then, one summer day, while he was working in the fields, he hung his coat over the hedge. While he farmed she furtively pulled the hidden object out of his pocket. It was she now who gasped at 'this thing'; and at last, relieved, sighed, 'Ach, it's only an old woman.'

I look in the mirror and, of course, know it is not my father. And I am amused by the Martian response of the Blasket Island farmer. William James though, in his *Papers on Philosophy*, cautions me not to make patronising judgements of other people's primitive or unsophisticated responses.

Hence the stupidity and injustice of our opinions, so far as they deal with the significance of alien lives. Hence the falsity of our judgements, so far as they presume to decide in an absolute way on the value of other person's conditions or ideals . . .

What queer disease is this that comes over you every day, of holding things and staring at them like that for hours together, paralysed of motion and vacant of all conscious life? The African savages came nearer the truth; but they, too, missed it when they gathered wonderingly round one of our American travellers who, in the interior, had just come into possession of a stray copy of the New York *Commercial Advertiser* and was devouring it column by column. When he got through, they offered him a high price for the mysterious object; and, being asked for what they wanted it, they said: 'For an eye medicine' – that being the only reason they could conceive of for the protracted bathe which he had given his eyes upon its surface.

The spectator's judgement is sure to miss the root of the matter, and to possess no truth. The subject judged knows a part of the world of reality which the judging spectator fails to see, knows more while the spectator knows less; and, wherever there is conflict of opinion and difference of vision, we are bound to believe that the truer side is the side that feels the more, and not the side that feels the less.

December 12th

Emma Mitchell of Random House, aware that I knew Bernice Rubens, has kindly sent me Bernice's posthumous memoir, *When I Grow Up*.

I first met Bernice when I was a schoolboy at St Illtyd's College and she attended the posher and more scholastic Cardiff High School for Girls. Her shining mischievous eyes stared at you, sized you up, from beneath a liquorice-black fringe which covered most of her forehead. She was a short teenager, one who frequently had a lopsided sardonic smile above her somewhat pointed chin. 'My mother knows your mother,' she informed me. We were both Jewish, both Welsh, though in her memoir Bernice Rubens judgementally insists, 'Dannie Abse, a Cardiffian like myself, but far more Welsh than I . . . his Jewishness strictly secondary.' I don't know about that. Perhaps Mrs Rubens told her daughter that my mother born in Ystalyfera spoke Welsh like others in that Swansea valley village, and that when Bernice attempted to enrol me in a Zionist youth movement I declined. As for religion, at sixteen I was happy to believe that when water spurts from a rock or a bush spontaneously bursts into flames it is time to consult a physician. But did that make me less of a Jew?

Years later when Bernice came to London I introduced her to her future husband Rudi Nassauer for which act, I believe, she never entirely forgave me. Not many years passed before Bernice found a reason to quarrel disharmoniously with Joan and me. As Emerson said, 'We boil at different degrees', and Bernice came to the boil early – even more so when Rudi eventually left her to live with another woman.

With advancing years, unhappy Bernice Rubens could be utterly waspish. Once, at a party given by Lewis and Nan Greifer, Mira H., a documentary film maker of renown, entered the room and greeted Bernice warmly. '*Go away*,' Bernice almost screamed, '*I don't like you.*' I remember how Mira turned to Joan and myself who happened to be standing by. 'What have I done?' Mira asked, her eyes wide, hurt.

In *When I Grow Up* Bernice relates how Rudi became a disciple of Canetti's and how this was disastrous for her relationship with her husband. 'It was during this time that a Mr Elias Canetti came into our life and seemed to lodge there permanently ... Mr Canetti had written one novel, *Auto da Fé*, which Rudi had read and was deeply impressed by ... My marital situation fascinates Canetti ... He moves around Hampstead couples and lovers doling out destructive advice and waiting, with infinite pleasure, for the shit to hit the fan.'

There is a touching conclusion to Bernice's memoir. She relates how finally, in Rudi's ill and lonely months of life, she visited him. 'He had mellowed considerably and he showed me a kindness that in the past he could not have afforded ... as the years pass, I can recall with greater ease the good and happy times we spent together, and in their shadow the dark years fade.'

Then

During the post-war years it was Rudi who had literary ambitions, not Bernice. She had, as far as I know, no thought of becoming an author. At that time I think she invested her hope of fame in Rudi's future success. Even before Bernice came to live in London Rudi would read to me his incomprehensible poems in a booming, cathedral-slow Dylan Thomas voice, mesmerising himself with its cadences and repetition. 'Listen to this,' he commanded me, I'm going to call it "Song of the Prodigal Son to His Mother".'

Song of the Prodigal Son to his Mother

. . . Ago in a yesterday, May of a yesterday,
your son, your man, drumming summation
in his chance, sensed you sensual
leaving you, leaving you, tree in ear,
feet of roots and wingèd seeds,
leaving you. You.

After finishing reading the poem and allowing the suitable reverence of a hush he would say almost puzzled, 'Wasn't that wonderful?' I was twenty-three years of age, aware of Nietzsche's sneer about the poets of his day, 'they muddy their own waters so as to appear more deep' – but I wasn't sure. Rudi was so confident about his own talent and his poetry-reading voice would have beguiled a listener even if he declaimed aloud the telephone directory. Besides, the ear was often in autocratic charge of my own early poetry. So?

In 1946 Rudi and I both had books of poems accepted for publication. *Poems* by Rudolf Nassauer appeared first and Rudi excitedly told me his book would be featured on the BBC's prestigious *Third Programme*. 'Would you come around my place and listen to it?' he asked. 'I'm going to invite a few other close friends.'

I remember sitting next to Emanuel Litvinoff as Roy Fuller began a talk about 'How Not to Write a Poem'. He spoke of the malevolent influence of Dylan Thomas on young poets and then, after a recitation of one of Rudi's worst poems:

> ... All is oneness ever ever
> above, above, above, above,
> (flesh in the tie of dive coronation
> rope of the sea-king's people fear and urge
>
> bound to the stake of pain
> Oneness, oneness, oneness, oneness
> orb o sceptic
> animal of gold ...

he tore Rudi's book into pieces, calling it all counterfeit. I glanced across the funereal room at Bernice's baleful downcast face. She too had heard Rudi recite in magisterial voice his poetry and since she must have been in love with him then, expected his work to be fit to join the hagiographa, or at least for Rudi to be hailed and that we his friends would vocally jubilate.

We all sat there discomfited. Someone switched off the radio, and after consolatory responses from us all, we unsmiling quit the room of humiliation, one by one. I must confess I thought of my own book soon to be published and of Dylan Thomas's influent power perhaps on it.

Roy Fuller's review had been merciless. He did quote the worst of Rudi's poetry as I have done – an easy target; but there was latent talent in Rudi's work for a less severe critic to have fathomed. Alas, Rudi never published a poem again. He turned to prose, wrote two novels, before Bernice blossomed into an author who would win the Booker Prize.

December 13th

Six months since the accident on the M4 and, as I remember this or think that, my eyes leak like a tap with a half-perished washer. I am, I feel, leading a posthumous life. I don't know myself. But now Goethe's remark comes to mind: 'Know myself? If I knew myself I'd run away.'

Outside in our back garden, individual leaves decorate the trees. Frost on the grass. Leaves on the frost. Sun trailing through morning's mist.

December 15th

Ten days to Christmas and only now do I hear that the woman driver of the Mini Cooper which unaccountably crashed into the back of our car that night on the M4 is to be prosecuted. I can still hear her voice crying, 'I'm sorry, I'm sorry,' as I gaze down at my dead wife. Still no inquest. Legal matters rumble on so slowly. Sorry? She said she was sorry!

December 17th

On Radio 3 they are broadcasting a season of music by Bach and not for the first time that composer's undeniable potency induced in me an associative response. I was transported back in time to a spacious large church in Venice which Joan and I had entered in order to view certain paintings by Veronese. Because a service was going on we moved behind the broad pillars quietly, in the shadows, not wishing to draw attention to ourselves. We did not heed the priest or the responses of the sparse congregation; but concentrated on our secular visual purpose.

Then, startled, we heard the violin, the soaring music of one violin pure and serious and eloquent. We sat down on wooden chairs captivated by the solo sonata. Rilke called such music 'the breathing of statues'. In that half-dark calm space, enclosed by solemn stone, we listened entranced to the soul of Bach.

Music, classical and popular, evokes for all of us from time to time an occasional Proustian remembrance. The legend I like best about music and nostalgia was related to me by my friend Peter Vansittart. It concerns a Chinese general defending a city being besieged by the Mongols and who, no food, no hope left, knew that the next day he would have to surrender. That moonlit night for the last time he climbed the battlement to view the Mongols encamped around the city. From the high wall he saw the vast number of their tents stretching on the plain below the moon and the stars. Then the general played on his pipe, played the most lonely, the most forlorn and desolate melodies beloved by the Mongols. The enemy soldiers roused, heard the music and were moved. By dawn they had become utterly homesick and departed.

In fact, rather than in legend, did that historical story have such a conveniently happy Hollywood ending?

History

(*To Peter Vansittart*)

The last war-horse slaughtered and eaten
long ago. Not a rat, not a crow-crumb
left; the polluted water scarce;
the vile flies settling on the famous
enlarged eyes of skeleton children.

Tonight the moon's open-mouthed. I must
surrender in the morning. But those
cipher tribes out there, those Golden Hordes,
those shit! They'll loot and maim and rape.
What textbook atrocities in the morning?

Now, solitary, my hip-joint aching,
half-lame, I climb the high battlements
carrying a musical instrument.
Why not? What's better? The bedlam of sleep
or the clarities of insomnia?

Look! Below, most fearful perspective:
cloud-fleeing shadows of unending
flatlands; enemy tent after tent

pegged to the unstable moonlight.
You'd think the moon, exposed, would howl.

Besieged city, in some future
history book (aseptic page or footnote)
they'll fable your finale: how
your huck-shouldered, arthritic General,
silhouette on the dark battlements,

played on his pipe a Mongolian song,
an enemy song, played so purely
the Past disrobed, memory made audible,
(sharp as a blade, lonely, most consequent,
that soul-naked melody of the steppes);

how, below, the Mongol soldiers awoke,
listened, leaned on their elbows tamed,
became so utterly homesick, wretched,
so inflamed, that by the cold sweats
of dawnlight, they decamped, departed.

Ha! Such a pleasing, shameless story,
to be told over and over by these
and by those: by propagandists of music;
by descendants of the Mongols.
But, alas, only a scribe's invention.

The truth? I play pianissimo
and not very well. The sleepers
in their tents sleep on, the sentries
hardly stir. I loiter on the battlements.
Stars! Stars! I put away my pipe and weep.

December 18th

I hesitate to go upstairs and enter Joan's study, but I wanted to find the manuscript of a book she had worked on years ago called *Journey into Art*. Because it required many coloured reproductions of paintings etc., it did not secure a publisher at that time. Maybe now, with the advances in printing, her book may be more commercially acceptable?

Before I discovered the typed manuscript I came across a page torn out from the *Guardian* dated April 16th 2005 which Joan had put away in a drawer. From the headline I knew at once why Joan had kept it.

She had always been aware that one side of her family had, long ago, originated in the small Fair Isle (three miles long, one and a half miles wide) which lies, isolated, twenty-five miles from the Shetland mainland. Joan also learnt from her mother who was born in Aberdeen that the family might have some Spanish haemoglobin in their blood strain. 'Something to do with a ship from the Spanish armada been wrecked off the coast of Scotland,' she informed me. 'It's just a family story.' Here, though, in front of me is the torn-out page of the *Guardian* carrying an article about the Fair Isle. I quote: 'In 1588, *El Gran Grifton*, flagship of the Spanish armada was shipwrecked off Fair Isle. Its 300 sailors spent six weeks living with the islanders. Its wreck was discovered in 1970.'

I shall pass on this torn-out page to my grand-children. Meanwhile I wonder about those Spanish sailors scrambling out from the lashes of the waves,

then crawling over sea-sprayed rocks to reach breath-
lessly the sanctuary of the wind-blistering small bleak
island where the sparse population labour in silence.

And did the relatively few young women eye the
soaked foreigners with suspicion or welcome them with
sober Christian kindness? Given their probable religious
scruples was there brutal rape or when the apple was
ripe did they enjoy willing conjugation? Who knows?
QED ends the pleasure of speculation! I see a field on
which no one is walking. There is a story to be told
about the six-week stay of those Spanish sailors — a
novel, a play, a film script. Maybe, one day ... But
research would be needed and now there is no helpful
scholar in the house as there once was.

December 19th
Joan's manuscript, I discover, is over 400 pages long.
I'm surprised that it contains two contributions by
myself. Pieces I've forgotten about. More importantly,
Joan introduces us to scenes such as Freud transfixed
in front of Michelangelo's Moses, Ruskin crushed by
the might of Tintoretto, and Kokoschka moved to tears
by a sculpture in the Medici Chapel. In her introduction she invites the reader to embark 'on a vicarious
journey through many of the art galleries in Western
Europe in the company of a lively, varied group of
people — artists, writers, musicians, and, indeed, some
with no artistic bent at all. Each one, of whatever time
or century, has written an account of his or her
encounter with a certain work of art. The journey starts

in London, and ends, after visits to more than a score of galleries, in Madrid . . .'

Joan also remarks on the strange sensations that can be engendered in confronting a painting or sculpture: the fancy that you breathe where the artist breathed, you look where he looked. Nathaniel Hawthorne touched the unfinished bas-relief by Michelangelo in the Uffizi 'because it seemed as if he might have been at work on it only an hour ago'.

'We may not all have shared such a memorable conjunction before a picture,' Joan wrote, 'but besides the consciousness of the "ghostly" presence of the artist at work it is possible to speculate on those who have stood there before us: how did they feel, what did they say? The gallery is full of echoes of concentrated attention and by our indulgence in this kind of necromancy we can achieve an almost palpable sense of human continuity.'

In Joan's study I put down the manuscript that I have just been reading and quoting from and, for a suspended moment, look at the empty chair before Joan's desk.

December 21st

Keren has decided to stay in Ogmore immediately after Xmas. 'Come with me,' she said. I find it difficult enough entering Joan's study upstairs, never mind visiting the haunted familiars of our house in Ogmore.

Maybe in 2006 I shall enjoy again the oxygen walks from Ogmore to Southerndown. To misquote Shelley, there is only one better walk in the world than from

Ogmore to Southerndown and that is the walk from Southerndown to Ogmore. Meanwhile, I imagine strolling down to the beach and listening to the sound of the waves' irregularities, to the sssh of the shingle and the shuffling and the sizzling of the sand when the waves recede. This time of year, though, Ogmore may show its rarer, more bleak side as I recalled in my diary of 1993.

Then
The wind has gone mad. An hour ago, as I bent forward through the blinding wind to the village Post Office store, the sun, indifferent, keeping its own obsessional time, sank lower towards the small quivering shore-hills of Somerset. Some minutes later, carrying the *South Wales Echo* and a bottle of refrigerator-cold milk, I walked back, my fingers freezing, my eyes still watering, in this lunatic gale. The telegraph wires howled like BBC radio sound-effects for a play about a havoc storm at sea.

Looking out towards Somerset, I thought how I would dread being out there on a bucking ship in that fairground, switch-back, elephant-grey Bristol Channel. Not that one single boat was visible. Indeed, nobody appeared to inhabit the numb, land-locked afternoon either. Ogmore seemed nerveless, deserted. Some sheep huddled behind a stone-armoured wall, a few separate silhouettes of seagulls were flung off course, lifted giddily wide and high against the sky, and an idiot tin can, animated by the relentless wind, scraped the macadam as it bucketed past me, its sound diminishing with each step I took.

Though it was still afternoon, the lamp posts began to glow. Soon it will be the shortest day of the year. Tomorrow we return to London. This will be our last sojourn in Ogmore this 1993. And, somehow, when I open our wooden gate, I had that old familiar sense of something ending, 1993 going out as I was coming in. Perhaps it was something to do with the impending early darkness and the fury of the wind — something like a regretful *au revoir*, a smileless valediction, an end of a book also which, however, possesses a few blank pages after the print has run out. The coalhouse door was flapping and I bolted it tight. Inside the safe house the wind was defeated despite the rattling windows. It is now night outside. The river, unseen, drifts into the glutted sea, the scarce ghost-stars wheel about the dark poles of the sky.

December 22nd

Christmas cards keep on coming. A number from friends in South Wales such as Tony Curtis and Cary Archard. They scribble notes asking how I am; and I think of another friend, the American poet Stanley Moss who remarked, 'night is always present, sunlight is the guest'. But I'm OK. I'm coping. I'm limping along. I miss Joan.

December 23rd

A great commotion in the street outside our front room. I look through the window and note how two cars in the middle of the road are at a curious angle to each other. Neither seems damaged, but the two men, presumably the two drivers, appear to be quarrelling. One is gesticulating wildly. I can't hear what he's saying, but I guess he's swearing like billyo.

It seems obscene words have their social uses – their articulation may not merely precede violent action but become a substitute for it. The latter proves to be the case because soon the two men retire to their cars and drive away out of my life while I think that if only Cain and Abel had known a few choice swear words the first fratricide might never have taken place.

Then
Our house in South Wales during the 1930s was almost oath free. My mother never shouted in anger anything less refined than 'damn it!' or 'Helen of Troy!' or 'dirty dog'. My father also declined to allow himself at home the improper consolations of a barrack-room vocabulary. At worst he would growl, 'Adolf bloody 'itler'.

As for me, my explorations at seven years of age into uttering forbidden words was wilfully accidental. I remember Dai Davies pulling Alun Williams's nose and yelling, 'you count.' Some weeks later my brother Leo had pushed me and I rapped my head against the fender. 'You count,' I yelled at him. Quietly but vehemently he made me promise never never never to use that word again. Evidently it was a secret word, one perhaps that could summon horned demons into the room. How did Dai Davies come to know this dangerous code word? Anyway, I promised Leo never to speak 'count' again, not even in the peculiar way he, my fourteen-year-old brother pronounced it. Over the years I have never used the word without feeling I have broken a holy promise and betrayed myself.

And Then

We visited the poet Vernon Watkins in August 1956. He invited Joan and me for tea at his house perched on a Gower Coast cliff. He, a most proper man, treated my visit with great old-fashioned courtesy, and certainly would not use 'count' or any lesser swear word in front of Joan. So he had some difficulty when he told us how angry he was with Faber who were about to publish the letters that he had received from his friend, Dylan Thomas. It seemed they had censored Dylan's four letter words.

'Now one word,' raged Vernon, 'Dylan used frequently. He used it quite innocently not only in his letters. This word,' he glanced at my wife uneasily, 'is often used these days and Faber have no right to censor ... um ... this word.' Vernon looked down at the floor. 'Many people who speak this, er, word are not necessarily ill-bred. Besides, readers nowadays are accustomed to read ...' He rotated his head a little so that my wife's ankles and shoes must have confronted him '... To read the ... quite common word.'

And Then and Then

Seven years after our visit to see Vernon Watkins I wrote a one act play, *Gone*, which had several productions and eventually interested Southern Television. However

I refused to allow it to be broadcast because they wished to censor it too stupidly. They wrote to my agent, Peggy Ramsey: 'we can allow Mr Abse only one "bloody" per half-hour.'

Later, when *Gone* was broadcast on Radio 3, the lead actor, Alfred Marks, found it natural to garnish the text with even a few more 'bloodys' than I had written in.

December 25th

I went to Paul and Susanna's home in Muswell Hill for our annual family Christmas lunch. I observed that Keren was wearing Joan's amber necklace. Tomorrow Paul and Susanna journey north to spend time with Paul's ageing parents; Keren goes to Ogmore, and David and Kitty travel to France for a brief holiday.

I drove back before the too early appointment of darkness. The streets this Christmas Day were oddly empty. Little traffic, fewer people, shut shops, and I thought of the American dramatist George Ade who described his visit to London on Christmas Day circa 1930: 'A soft gloom covered the earth. The sky was a sombre canopy, compromising between a grey and a dun. If you should mix battleship colours with the shade used in painting refrigerator cans, you might get an approximation of the effect. The light came from nowhere. Not freezing weather but in the sluggish air a chill which cut through top coats ... As we walked forth that Christmas we found the metropolis of the world had become merely an emptiness of walls and shutters. If machine guns had been planted at Trafalgar Square to sweep each radiating thoroughfare, there would have been no fatalities.'

December 27th
Phone call from Keren. She walked down to the beach and thought of summer and of that extraordinary afternoon when I and she listened to the choral singing from the people sitting on the rocks.

Then
Keren was seven years of age and she wanted to paddle. There were few people, less than fifty, scattered here and there on different rocks, or spread out on brightly coloured towels on the sand or on the sloping grey-blue pebbles that resembled, from the distance, sleeping pigeons. All was quiet but for the whisper of the waves that collapsed gently against Keren's small legs and my relatively big feet. The sun threw its ceaseless silver arrows into the sea while our shoes and socks lay some twenty-two yards away, a cricket pitch away, on the sand. Suddenly, for no evident reason, one person began to sing in Welsh. Another person took it up and then another. Soon most of the people on the beach, many presumably strangers to each other, sang harmoniously and with resonant yearning, 'Ar hyd y nos.' It could have been a phoney scene from some second-rate film about Wales. But this was real — no commercial tourist hogwash suggesting Wales was 'The Land of Song'.

January 1st 2006

Shall I continue this journal through 2006? Though I am talking to myself, like other diarists, I also presuppose another reader. I have been a professional author for all my adult life. Writing is what I do and I know it is a writer's job to address others however few there may be. Yet I understand Virginia Woolf when she scolded herself for 'the lawless exercise of writing diaries' instead of confronting the more difficult task of working on a new novel. I haven't written a poem since I began this, therapeutic for me, journal.

Dylan Thomas used to hoard a Mars bar in his Austin 7 garage—study at the back of the Boathouse in Laugharne so that he had something to look forward to next morning. I sometimes think my appointment with the next page of this journal/anthology is my Mars bar alternative.

Sad? Pathetic? As a doctor I know I'm not entirely well because happy memories that should make me smile do not do so. On the contrary. I'm never far from tears. I think of these lines from Henry King's exequy for his dead wife, Anne, who died in 1624 (see Appendix Two):

> Sleep my love in the cold bed
> Never to be disquieted!
> My last good night! Thou wilt not wake
> Till I thy fate shall overtake
> Till age, or grief, or sickness must
> Marry my body to that dust
> It so much loves ...

January 6th

At the oldest coffee house in London, 'The Coffee Cup' in Hampstead, I asked Milein Cosman this morning if she had ever drawn herself. 'Not really,' she said. 'Why not?' I queried. 'Because I'm always available,' she replied.

I thought of Rembrandt who from his earliest years had portrayed himself twice a year. Surely not because he was merely available? Perhaps he recognised he was never the same man twice. All of us are, as it were, temporary people passing through. And as we look in the mirror not only do our faces gradually alter but our perceptions change too. I daresay an artist's self-regard may be considered as investigative narcissism but any man with half a mind will sooner than later need to ask questions about what is existence and the most profound question should be addressed to himself. Rembrandt looking at the canvas on his easel declared, 'Here I am, the Dutchman who has never been to Italy, the greatest living master of form.' But Rembrandt's self-portraits say more than that. They are themselves existential probings.

Writers offer their self-portraits in autobiographies, memoirs, journals, while novelists, the defective ones, through their novels. (The better the novel the more unknowable the character of the novelist.) Poets, too, sometimes with deliberation take as subject matter themselves.

Some in their solipsistic self-regardings may, like Rembrandt, boast of their prowess (I'm the greatest living master of form) or of their work, forgoing the virtue of reticence. Walt Whitman, for instance, in his

'Song for Myself' – 'I find no sweeter fat than sticks
to my bones.' But most compose their self-portraits
with a lighter ~~self~~-deprecating air: 'How unpleasant to
meet Mr Eliot / With his features of clerical cut.' One
self-profile I enjoy is by the South African poet, David
Wright, who alas died a few years ago and whose work
is shamefully neglected. David Wright, since the age of
seven, had been completely deaf following a vicious
bout of meningitis.

Funeral Oration

Composed at thirty, my funeral oration: here lies
David John Murray Wright, 6′ 2″, myopic blue
    eyes;
Hair grey (very distinguished-looking, so I am told);
Shabbily dressed as a rule, susceptible to cold;
Acquainted with what are known as the normal
    vices;
Perpetually short of cash; useless in a crisis;
Preferring cats, hated dogs; drank (when he could)
    too much;
Was deaf as a tombstone; and extremely hard to
    touch.
Academic achievements: B.A., Oxon (2nd class);
Poetic: the publication of one volume of verse,
Which in his thirtieth year attained him no fame at
    all
Except among intractable poets, and a small
Lunatic fringe congregating in Soho pubs.
He could roll himself cigarettes from discarded
    stubs,

Assume the first position of yoga; sail, row, swim;
And though deaf, in church appear to be joining a
    hymn.
Often arrested for being without a permit,
Starved on his talents as much as he dined on his
    wit,
Born in a dominion to which he hoped not to go
    back
Since predisposed to imagine white possibly black:
His life, like his times, was appalling; his conduct
    odd;
He hoped to write one good line; died believing in
    God.

Then

Over the years I used to meet David Wright regularly
in one of the Soho pubs. He was able to lip-read
much of what I said though often we had to resort
to notes on scraps of paper. Late in life he lived in
Portugal and would visit London every six months. I
recall our last lunch together. Our conversation, as
usual, tended to be desultory but reasonably serious.
Because of his deafness it was laborious to relate a
long philosophical peroration or an extended
humorous anecdote.

That lunchtime both David and I agreed that there
was no such thing as a bad poem. He had quoted
Wordsworth who venerated that Poetry, if it is not more
than very well, it is very bad and that there is no inter-
mediate state. And I told David about Sir Adolph
Abrahams, a consultant at Westminster Hospital when

I had been a medical student. Sir Adolph had an aversion to the word 'slight' or 'slightly'. If a student at a ward round happened to diagnose that a patient had a slight lump, Sir Adolph Abrahams, who always searched for the absolute, would flush into raw pink flesh and shout, 'Slight? SLIGHT? It's either a lump or not a lump, boy. A woman is pregnant or not – never *slightly* pregnant.'

January 7th

As usual woke up too early. And, unusually, remembered my dream: Joan was absent because she didn't love me any more. In the darkness I, an old man, found myself crying and once again accused myself of self-pity.

January 8th

Susanna knowing that from time to time, when I haven't anything better to write, I find myself doodling aphorisms in my workbook, brought with her Don Paterson's recent publication, *The Book of Shadows*. Don Paterson offers sensible advice, 'Reading a book of aphorisms diligently in the sequence they appear makes about as much sense as eating a large jar of onions diligently in the sequence they appear; and it should go without saying that no one should try and finish either in one sitting.' So after an hour or so of browsing through his book I take his advice and write, instead, at this desk.

I've always been fond of aphorisms and proverbs.

One of my favourite volumes is *The Faber Book of Aphorisms* edited by W. H. Auden and Louis Kronenberger. Let me quote half a dozen from its varied pages:

'Never to talk about oneself is a very refined form of hypocrisy.'

Nietzsche

'The music at a wedding procession always reminds one of the music of soldiers going into battle.'

Heine

'It is muddleheaded to say, I am in favour of this kind of political regime rather than that: what one really means is I prefer this kind of police.'

Cioran

'Coition is a slight attack of apoplexy.'

Democritus of Abdera

'When a father gives to his son, both laugh; when a son gives to his father, both cry.'

Yiddish Proverb

'The devil's boots don't creak.'

Scottish Proverb

When it comes to aphoristic sayings I enjoy their kernels of wisdom, their wit, their dogmatism, though sometimes the reverse of what they argue is as true. For instance, T. S. Eliot's 'humankind cannot bear very much reality', provokes me to grunt, 'Yes, sir, but humankind cannot bear very much unreality.'

My wife never approved of me writing aphorisms. 'Keep them for your poems,' she advised me, thinking they needed elaboration, context, form. She wouldn't have agreed with Don Paterson when he confesses, 'The aphorism is a brief waste of time, the poem is a complete waste of time. The novel is a monumental waste of time!' (What activity, Don, is not a waste of time?)

To publish aphorisms is a vulnerable act. So often the aphorist does not hit the target and then he or she just seems to be a clever fool. Paterson's book contains brief reflections on a love affair, on human conduct, on God, on Death, on Art, etc. and while some arrive at the central bullseye, e.g. 'We turn from the light to see' predictably others thud sententiously against the woodwork. Oh, the dogmatism of a judicious aphorism! It says to the reader, 'I am wise. I am dominant. Listen, put that in your pipe and smoke it!' When amusing, though less democratic and more universal, it can be close to a mere penetrating witticism. A witticism is different in that it is best when uttered spontaneously on a *singular* social occasion. It requires a situational context. I'm thinking, for example, of the composer, Korngold, who drafted into the Austrian Army during the First World War was ordered to write a March for the regiment. Later, he was summoned to the Commanding Officer's

Headquarters. 'This March is too fast,' the CO said, 'Yes, too fast, too fast, Korngold.' Unsmiling, Korngold responded, 'But sir . . . it's for the retreat, sir.'

Then

In January 2004 the literary magazine *Acumen* published the first of two sets of aphorisms that I had taken from my workbooks. By way of introduction I had begun with 'An aphorism should cast a shadow', so later when I saw the publishers, Picador, were promoting a book of aphorisms by Don Paterson titled *The Book of Shadows*, I wondered and was curious.

I knew Don Paterson a little. We had both been involved in a BBC programme broadcast from the Edinburgh festival so when I encountered Don at the annual T. S. Eliot Prize celebration at Lancaster House I asked him if he had seen the January issue of *Acumen*. Perhaps I shouldn't have done. Don responded amiably but blankly and said that his *Book of Shadows* had recently appeared and he would send me a copy. In return, I said I would send him a selection of my aphoristic doodles that had been published in *Acumen* (see Appendix Three). But he never did send me his book and, negligent, I never did post to him my doodles.

January 10th

I am, as much as any man, appeased into pleasurable benignity by subtle flattery and Q's compliments about my literary work are always intelligently sly. She is also, or can be, physically provoking. Last September when she visited London at our meeting she immediately kissed me on the mouth in a way that seemed to be more a signal than a greeting. The enthusiastic kiss and entrance was repeated today. Do I misread her? After the rituals of flirtation whatever carnal arousings I experienced were swiftly quelled when she mentioned Joan. I said nothing. What could I tell her about the obsessional and single-minded, tearful returning boomerang of grief? I've reluctantly become half-reconciled to my present ache of celibacy and so, finally, I asked after her husband! But on the way back from South End Green I thought of a poem called 'Misunderstanding' by the Canadian poet, Irving Layton. He wrote that when he made a pass at a woman by placing his hand on her thigh, she moved away. Layton concluded that her devotion to literature was not perfect!

January 11th

A letter from my lawyer. That is to say from the real world. She has notified the other driver's insurance company that she's commissioned a psychiatrist, a Dr T. Meehan, to report 'on my post-traumatic stress' and, at a later date, she will 'obtain evidence relating to my physical injuries'. I now must wait to be summoned to Dr Meehan's consulting room. I'd rather read Shakespeare.

Still no date for the inquest.

January 13th

I've not long returned from Sainsbury's to sit at this desk. Dreary, like my present mood, the London clouds do not move: it has been another cold grey-ceilinged morning. The few pedestrians about looked as if they had just emerged from a huge refrigerator and walked with their heads down.

Joan would have been amazed – knowing how I'm hardly self-reliant – at my almost efficient attempts to manage the household quotidian tasks: shopping, cooking (much dependence on the microwave) washing-up, etc. But these are boring menial matters and whom am I addressing?

Michael Faraday, that eminent physicist, in his electrically interesting journal felt uncomfortable to be addressing himself so he pretended that he was writing to his sister, Margaret. I too need to engage in a similar pretence so now invent a correspondent, sympathetic as Faraday's sister! I confess to her that I've discovered that when a man wakes up in a morning such as this, and cries (unseen of course) in abhorrent self-pity or otherwise, he is physiologically left depleted, untranquil, and for a while physically exhausted like one experiencing hypoglycaemia.

Perhaps, on such mornings I should, like Christopher (Kit) Wright, take the advice of Dr Coué who in the 1920s recommended that on waking one should chant, 'Every day in every way I grow better and better.'

When I get up in the morning
I thought the whole thing through:
Thought, who's the hero, the man of the day?
Christopher, it's you.

With my left arm I raised my right arm
High above my head:
Said, Christopher, you're the greatest.
Then I went back to bed.

I wrapped my arms around me,
No use counting sheep.
I counted legions of myself
Walking on the deep.

The sun blazed on the miracle,
The blue ocean smiled:
We like the way you operate,
Frankly, we like your style.

Dreamed I was in a meadow,
Angels singing hymns,
Fighting the nymphs and shepherds
Off my holy limbs.

A girl leaned out with an apple,
Said, you can taste for free.
I never touch the stuff, dear,
I'm keeping myself for me.

Dreamed I was in heaven
God said, Over to you,
Christopher, you're the greatest!
And Oh, it's true, it's true!

I like my face in the mirror
I like my voice when I sing.
My girl says it's just infatuation –
I know it's the real thing.

That verse by Kit Wright makes me smile – but I look out of the window and the static clouds over the rooftops opposite have darkened to the colour of statues.

January 17th
Apart from the usual disaster news – Iraq, and other daunting reports about similar organised crimes, paedophiles, broken marriages, delinquent juveniles, failing NHS hospitals, the hurdling oil prices, global warming, the racist undercurrents of our society, etc. – there was one unusual item in today's *Guardian* that also reminded me of the frightening comedy of human behaviour. It was about an African grey parrot which wrecked the two-year loving relationship of a certain Chris Taylor and a Suzy Collins.

It seemed that every time Suzy Collins's mobile rang the parrot, Ziggy, squawked out the name of Suzy's clandestine lover-on-the-side, Gary. Worse ensued. Ziggy began to call out, 'I love you, Gary,' and to make amorous kissing noises.

After the relationship, parrot-sabotaged, ended, Ziggy continued to repeat 'Gary . . . Gary . . .' until Chris could not bear it any longer and gave the parrot to a local avian dealer. 'I wasn't sorry to see the back of Suzy,' mourned Chris, 'but it really broke my heart to let Ziggy go.' For her part, Suzy observed, 'I'm surprised to hear he's got rid of that bloody bird. He spent more time talking to it than he did to me.'

This sad domestic incident made me think of that occasion when Lady Caroline Lamb's parrot bit her big toe. As she hopped about the room, her lover, Byron, somewhat macho, picked up the bird and hurled it against the wall whereupon the parrot screeched 'Johnny', leaving Lady Caroline pale and Byron wondering.

Beautiful married women of this world, take note of the danger of keeping a parrot as a pet. Dogs OK. Cats OK. Those dumb goldfish constantly chewing water, no problem. But parrots? Verboten. Gwaharddedig. Interdit. Prohibito. Vietato. Zakázano.

January 18th
The proceedings at the memorial celebration for Joan last November are now on a website David created (see Acknowledgements, p. 269). I read it through until I came to Cary Archard's articulate memory of Joan. 'When I think of Joan Abse,' Cary said, 'I see her, secateurs in hand, surrounded by colour in her garden at Ogmore-by-Sea with its wonderful mixture of flowers

in the beds between the privet and the cotoneaster hedges.'

I could not read on. I had to blink back tears because, suddenly, I too saw Joan as she was in the different seasons of the Ogmore garden. There was that time she called me to view the astonishing hordes of butterflies, mostly small blue ones, some larger white, circling and circling around the lavender bush. It was an epiphany. The bush was their idol and they were, in their pilgrim hundreds, paying homage to it. And then I could see Joan clearly cutting down the militant pink-red valerian, locally known as 'Devils Dung', which grow everywhere in Ogmore too profusely. And then I saw Joan lying flat on her stomach leaning over the goldfish pond as she plunged her bare arm into the water to pull out the rotting water lily leaves, the goldfish darting away.

It is January and extremely cold so perhaps the Christmas roses Joan always delighted in may still be thriving. Not too far away from those modest roses Joan's ashes lie.

January 21st

Surely not all of the old gods have been identified. Perhaps some were so awesome nobody dared to speak their name. I think the whale with its divine strength must have been one such. When Jonah went into the belly of the whale he prayed – but did he, in that dark abyss, address his prayer to the whale? The whale responded, sailed for the coast and vomited Jonah upon the dry land while the seagulls above circled and wailed. What thunder in the surf as that whale turned and returned to its deep mysterious feeding grounds.

Far from its North Atlantic home a bottle-nosed whale appeared in the Thames near the Palace of Westminster on Friday. Soon thousands of spectators stood on the bridges and along the embankments as rescue attempts led to the whale, in its afflictions, being loaded on to a barge. Slowly, slowly, the barge chugged downriver towards the opening up estuary. I could not help wondering whether the perplexed, stressed, sick mammal with its little chance of surviving should be put out of its misery.

Vets are trained like doctors to save life. I know how a doctor saving a seemingly dying patient can feel a sense of triumph. And should the patient die the doctor may feel sometimes utterly defeated. So it must be with vets. The heroic thing may be simply to help the patient to go more swiftly into irrevocable anaesthesia, to deny self-aggrandisement and the joy of triumph.

The pictures I've seen on TV of the rescue attempts remind me of an ancient text by a Persian sea captain:

Abu al-Hasan Muhammed told me he'd seen a monster fish stranded on the shore when the tide ebbed. When the tide turned the huge fish was dragged up as far as the town. The Amir, Ahmad b. Hilal, rode out accompanied by troops and the people came to see it. A horseman could enter its jaws and exit the other side without dismounting. They measured it: it was over 200 cubits long and its height about fifty cubits. The fat from its eyes was sold for 10,000 dirhams. The ship-master, Ismailawayh, says this fish — it's called a 'Wal' feeds in the Sea of Zanj and in the great Sea of Samarqand. It likes to wreck ships and sailors ward it off by striking pieces of wood together as they shout and beat drums. Sometimes it spouts water which rises up like a minaret ...

I find it interesting that the ancient scribes lacked a word for the whale. That Persian sea captain spoke of a 'monster fish'. The Bible, too, relates how Jonah was swallowed by 'a great fish'. The people of antiquity know only of whales through the fantastical tales of sailors. Those sea-monsters lived near the far myste-rious edge of the world.

We, of course, know so much more of whales but we still find them awesome creatures. People contem-plate existence when they observe the alien whale — as they might, at night, when in silent supplication they look up at the stars. Our curiosity has led tres-passing man even to record their mating love-cries, 'Songs of the Humpback Whale' became, decades ago, a best-selling Natural History LP. And their rhythmic serenades have been used by alternative 'healers' who claim that when their stressed turbulent patients listen to such recordings they are moved into a hypnotic tranquillity.

I now read in the *Guardian* that currently Japanese

vessels are pursuing 1,000 whales in the Southern oceans. The ironical trenchant conclusion of a poem by Tony Curtis comes to mind:

> Circling the fleet whales sing deeply
> Love to the hulls of factory ships.

January 22nd

After breakfast, 8.10 a.m. Through the windows I see the frost staying stubbornly on the grass. A cloudless sky, palest blue, and last night's ghostly swollen half-moon shaped like a rugby ball. Beneath it a silver line excreted by a gone aeroplane. Nearby, so many birds about this morning. In the bare branches of a neighbour's tall tree the silhouettes of two birds with long tails. Magpies. Two for joy?

On a Sunday morning like this Joan and I, when we were in London and not in Wales, would go for a walk in our local Golders Hill Park that climbs up to the wider Hampstead Heath. It's one of the most pleasant small parks of London and it's no surprise that so many of the wooden benches abound with the names of the dead who once loved to visit it – IN MEMORY OF ...

Ernest Rhys, the editor of the Everyman Library, along with friends such as Ezra Pound or W. H. Hudson, used to walk into Golders Hill Park. Until recently, before the foxes got them, one would see in the January pond near the walled flower garden beneath the willow tree, four flamingos standing one-legged on ice.

Walking in the park with Joan each time I saw these

flamingos I would recall W. H. Hudson's book about Patagonia, how he saw a huge congregation of flamingos, how one appeared more perfect, larger, more beautiful, than all the others. So W. H. Hudson shot it.

Then
It must have been the winter of 1980 when we returned from Ogmore-by-Sea to bring my mother here to stay with us for a while, that I wrote a poem, 'A Winter Visit', about her and Golders Hill Park with its little zoo, its gaudy peacocks etc.

Now she's ninety I walk through the local park
where, too cold, the usual peacocks do not screech
and neighbouring lights come on before it's dark.

Dare I affirm to her, so aged and so frail,
that from one pale dot of peacock's sperm
spring forth all the colours of a peacock's tail?

I do. But she like the sibyl says, 'I would die',
then complains, 'This winter I'm half dead, son.'
And because it's true I want to cry.

Yet must not (although only Nothing keeps)
for I inhabit a white coat not a black
even here — and am not qualified to weep.

So I speak of small approximate things,
of how I saw, in the park, four flamingos
standing, one legged on ice, heads beneath wings.

January 23rd

Another Monday. Slow days, fast weeks.

I came down to my study after my morning bath to keep my appointment with this diary/journal/anthology. I'm glad to do so and reread what I wrote yesterday about my mother in her old age. I'm reminded of a Talmudic story about a very old woman who visited Rabbi Jose ben Halafta. She complained, 'I don't want to live. I've no appetite for food or drink and my body aches with its heavy age.'

'Have you no interest in life at all?' asked the Rabbi.

'I go every day to the synagogue. That's my sole interest.'

'Then,' sighed the Rabbi, 'if you're certain you don't want to continue living give up that daily interest as well.'

The old woman ceased going to synagogue, and on the third day she sickened and died.

Of course writing these ephemeral pages is not my sole interest but the way I feel at present I, as a physician, know that to cease adding to it would not be the best thing for my well-being.

January 24th

Last night's dream. I woke up soon after 3 a.m. remembering my dream. Joan was behind the lavatory door and I kept on asking, 'Are you all right, Joan?' I heard, in reply, only a garbled murmur. My first conscious thought was to relate the dream back through the decades when we were young, before our children had been born. Joan had suffered a miscarriage and I was, in reality, outside the lavatory door asking the same question: 'Are you all right, Joan?' Then my second clear thought brought the dream in nearer focus to the night of the accident on the M4 when again I had cried out 'Are you all right, Joan' and had received no reply.

January 26th

I had not intended to go to the launch of the new edition of *Poems on the Underground* but Siân Williams offered to pick me up and drive me to Lauderdale House. I could not help recalling the last time I'd been there. This time, though, it was a convivial occasion – the publisher was particularly happy. *Poems on the Underground* had so far sold almost half a million copies.

After the speeches, Judith Chernaik, one of the editors of the anthology, invited Adrian Mitchell, Ruth Padel, Wendy Cope, etc. to read their poems from the book and since I was there Judith whispered to me that I should read 'Mysteries', my contribution to the anthology.

Mysteries

At night, I do not know who I am
when I dream, when I am sleeping.

Awakened, I hold my breath and listen:
a thumbnail scratches the other side of the wall.

At midday I enter a sunlit room
to observe the lamplight on for no reason.

I should know by now that few octaves can be heard,
that a vision dies from being too long stared at;

that the whole of recorded history even
is but a little gossip in a great silence;

that a magnesium flash cannot illumine,
for one single moment, the invisible.

I do not complain. I start with the visible
and am startled by the visible.

I had not read 'Mysteries' aloud for many years and I
was glad to renew acquaintance with it!

Last June I cancelled all my forthcoming readings
but I've agreed to do so again when my book *Running
Late* appears in early April. Siân Williams has arranged
for me to read on April 5th at the British Library and
Emma Mitchell, the PR at Hutchinson, is negotiating
other readings near the publication date, including one,
she hopes, at Hay-on-Wye. It will be strange to give
readings again without Joan participating or applauding
from the sidelines!

When I was leaving Lauderdale House with Siân,
John Rety stopped me. John may be a likeable innocent, a master chess player, but gazing at attractive Siân
Williams he said to me with momentary stupidity, 'So
you've got over it, then.' I could not help uncontrol-
lably, vehemently, replying, 'I'll never get over it, John.'
And I know, that whatever comes, whatever will be, that
is absolutely true.

Then

I was in Hay-on-Wye to give a reading. I arrived early and so had time to investigate the many second-hand bookshops of the small town. In the window of one of them I saw one of my out-of-print books, a first edition of *Way Out in the Centre*, published in 1981. It was reasonably priced and since I owned only one tired copy I decided to buy it. At the cashier's counter the young man who took my money said, 'It's signed you know.' I opened the book and saw my own signature on the flyleaf! The young cashier then said, trying to reassure me, 'We haven't charged much extra, sir. Abse signs easily.' I thanked him and left.

January 29th

Last night the Mozart celebration on Radio 3 migrated to television. On BBC 4 I caught glimpses of Sir Simon Rattle conducting the Berlin Philharmonic Orchestra. During the slower celestial plangencies of Mozart, Sir Simon's cherubic imbecile smile reminded me of one of those saints depicted in great paintings whose expression suggests a spiritual or post-coital serenity.

In his book, *Crowds and Power*, Elias Canetti speaks (masterfully!) of the fascism of the conductor, how the conductor has the power of life and death over the voices of the instruments (see Appendix Four). The conductor is the absolute dictator: the orchestra his enslaved obeying courtiers, the immediate audience his subjects. As Canetti asserts, 'His hands decree and prohibit. His ears search out profanation.' In brief, the conductor is omniscient and of course he enjoys the exercise of his power. Subtly, the signs of that pleasure must surely settle in the sublime expressions on the conductor's — Sir Simon Rattle's — face?

How close are musical and mystical enchantments? Mystics are reluctant to describe their experiences lest it diminish them. I suppose it was the same reason why Stendhal advised those who are happy not to describe the nature of their happiness. But I think, hope (without confidence) that to articulate unhappiness *is* to diminish it. A consolation. We all need to be consoled some of the time and some find it in music, some in religion, some in sex. And some in writing journals such as this. Take comfort, the Welsh language poet Gwyn Thomas, advises

> Even if you only grow onions,
> Breed rabbits or put ships in bottles,
> If that grips you, you are one of the saved . . .

Nietzsche declared that even the thought of suicide is a great consolation. It helps you to get through the night!

February 2nd

After a disorientated moment on waking I found myself in tears. It wasn't true. Joan was dead. Joan wasn't planning a holiday for us both.

I knew the origin of the dream. Yesterday I visited Leo who told me when his wife, Marjorie, died, he travelled abroad, went here, went there, to places where he and Marjorie had never been together. 'You should do the same,' he said. 'Not brood away in your house in Golders Green. I understand why you do not want to go to Ogmore at present. But you should allow yourself to be open to new impressions that travelling abroad can provide.'

Leo is now eighty-eight and he looks more shrunken, more fragile. Because he is so deaf I can no longer enjoy our usual lancinating arguments, our expressions of chronic sibling rivalry! It's more monologue than dialogue. If I do attempt to elaborate on a metaphor he has to turn to his young caring wife, Ania, whose lips he can read.

His knappish propensity to analyse everybody, like phosphorus spontaneously bursting into flames, led him to advise me to assuage my guilt which is the common consequence of new and especially sudden bereavement. 'But I don't feel guilty,' I replied too close to tears, remembering what happened. 'How can I feel guilty when I was driving in the slow lane preparing to leave the motorway when that other lethal wild car smashed into me from behind?'

True, now having to cope domestically for myself, and aware of how much Joan undertook to housework as well as to succour my demanding needs without complaint I realise I could have helped her more, and made more space for her. But that's hardly a confession of a profound guilt that others might suggest lies in the fougasse of the unconscious. Joan, I'm sure, was a happy woman. We were a happy couple – more than one, less than two.

Leo revealed that he has finished his book on Daniel Defoe. Probably he has mined, in the pit of Defoe's unconscious, sexual proclivities that would have startled the author himself, and no doubt, when it is published, will make Defoe scholars irate. Now he has begun to look through his psychoanalytical spectacles at the antics of biblical characters. 'You know who Jubal is?' he asked me. When I jubilated, 'Of course, he's the supposed inventor of the flute and the lyre,' Leo appeared to be somewhat disconcerted.

Joan once remarked with some irritation that Leo always seemed surprised when I could discuss matters beyond the province of poetry. 'He patronises you,' she objected. I didn't mind. After all, when I was ten and he a precocious sixteen, every Saturday morning in our house in South Wales, he would read out loud the quiz questions printed in the *News Chronicle*. Inerudite, of course, I didn't know the answers. 'You don't know *that*,' he would accuse me. 'You're so ignorant.'

It was always so, I suppose, the youngest in the family being chided by elder siblings. Evidence of it is there in the history books, in the Bible too, and in those legends that begin, 'Once upon a time, there was a king who had three sons. Two were intelligent but the youngest was stupid and called Dummling.' Ah, but Dummling wins through in the end, helped by a magical toad or white cat and on the last page scoops not only the prize but the Fair Lady. And didn't I 'scoop' Joan?

Then

Whatever heat generated by our fraternal rivalry I've long appreciated how much I owe to my elder brothers. Over the decades Wilfred and Leo have not only been concerned about my well-being but have allowed me influent intellectual gifts. Their generosity began as soon as I was born. Leo wrote in an autobiographical piece:

> I remember well the details of that fateful day although I was only six years five months old. With my eight-year-old brother Wilfred, I had, for reasons then obscure to me, been dispatched to another part of the city to stay with my maternal grandparents. This was more than acceptable to me since I was the favourite of my grandfather, a Talmudist who, I claim, was the first man to speak Welsh with a Yiddish accent. It was less congenial to my brother but, since he was the favourite of my paternal grandmother, a German born belligerent atheist, a woman of the Enlightenment, who lived but a few hundred yards away from the Talmudist, Wilfred was not over-fretful. The excursion would give both of us a full opportunity to play off the grandparents who, until their deaths, competed with each other for the grandchildren: we never failed to exploit the splendid opportunities that gave ever-increasing pocket money as the grandfather and grandmother over-trumped each other.
>
> After a few days sojourn we were told we could return home and that we would find there a splendid present, a new baby brother, who, my grandfather told me, would be called Daniel and who, my grandmother,

ever resenting the Biblical resonances, told me would be called Dannie. Well augmented with ninepence from the respective grandparents, we commenced our long walk home. I doubt if we were aware of the tale of the Magi and we certainly were not guided by any stars on our journey; but we decided after much discussion that we must arrive with a gift. We quickly reached agreement as to the nature of our presentation; no silly geegaw for us. What the new brother must have was reading material, for in Wales, unlike England, the term intellectual is not pejorative and we were brought up, too, in a Jewish ethos which taught us that in the beginning was the Word. But Wilfred and I fell out as to what reading material was suitable.

I wanted to take him, for instruction on the wider world, *The Children's Newspaper*, an Arthur Mee publication of which, as became a future politician, I was an avid reader; but Wilfred thought a coloured comic was more suitable, a choice which doubtless the future Emeritus Professor of psychiatry anticipated would stimulate the imagination of the child. In the end, with our pocket money, we bought both. When my turn came to enter my brother's bedroom and I saw the sleeping babe I became afflicted with doubt about his capacity to appreciate my gift; but my mother reassured me and told me that Dannie would enjoy it when he was awake. Now I think my mother deceived me and my present was not passed on.

Later Leo taught me to side with the Red Indians not the Cowboys, that the alphabet began with A stands for armaments the Capitalists' pride, B stands for

Bolshie the thorn in their side ... And later still I would see my eighteen-year-old brother standing on a 1930s soapbox in Llandaff Fields shouting something like: 'What we have here in Cardiff is a sluggish do-nothing Council led by purblind and rigid Tory patricians who, in turn, are served by unimaginative and timorous bureaucrats. Meanwhile we see more and more listless men, half a million in Wales alone, men without hope, ill-cared for, ill-clothed, ill-fed, their families desperate...' Afterwards, back home, Leo quoted lines I remember to this day: 'It's given to man to live but once, and he should so live that dying he may say, all my life, all my strength have been given to the finest cause in the world, the enlightenment and liberation of mankind.'

Leo's political skills are well-known, not least because of his reforming zeal while a member of parliament over two decades. Michael Foot once said to me, 'Leo did more to raise the quality of life for many in Britain through his private bills concerning divorce and homosexuality etc., than the government did under Wilson's long tenancy at 10 Downing Street.'

Leo's literary gifts, though, are less celebrated despite the publication of several insightful books such as *Wotan, My Enemy*. Before he reached the age of twenty he had already won first prize in an essay competition sponsored by a Sunday newspaper. I remember how I, some fourteen years of age, mightily impressed, had complained to Leo, 'I only get eight out of ten for my weekly essay at school.' It didn't matter what care I took, what the subject, my blue exercise book invariably was returned to me with Mr Graber's mark of eight out of ten. Leo generously offered to help me gain a higher mark. Scrupulously he wrote out my next essay and I, with confidence, copied it in my own handwriting. He made linguistic excursions I would not have dared. I was certainly grateful to Leo for his concern and talent and when the exercise book was handed back to me I read how I was now given seven out of ten! Beneath the essay, in red ink, Mr Graber wrote, 'Boy, do not use words you cannot understand.'

During the long tournament of our fraternal rivalry that incident has been my one and only victory.

February 3rd

My granddaughter, Larne, came for lunch. She informed me that Paul, her father who is a travel writer of some renown has taken her young brother, Max, on a skiing holiday in Colorado. Paul is doing a piece for a daily newspaper. Larne unlike Max is not keen on daring the snowy slopes.

'It's rather a Sisyphus exercise,' I remark. 'This ascending and descending again and again.'

Larne looks puzzled. I explain how Sisyphus was condemned by the gods to always heave a huge boulder up a mountainside until it reaches the summit. Then the boulder always rolls back so that Sisyphus has to descend and begin this task again. As Longfellow wrote:

With useless endeavour
Forever, forever,
Is Sisyphus rolling
His stone up the mountain,

'Besides skiing is a dangerous sport,' I continued. 'In 1968, during the Vietnam War, I went on a poetry-reading tour to the West Coast of the USA. When in Eugene, Oregon, I saw so many young people on crutches, so many casualties of the Vietnam War, I assumed; but I was soon disabused. "They've all been in the mountains skiing," I was told.'

After Larne left I thought how my days seem more and more Sisyphus-like. Waking in bed each morning to seize awareness, only to engage in the small prose of mundane things beginning with the washing of last night's cooking utensils! The repetition of it all! The boredom! And yet there are thankfully, unexpected permutations and variations – the letter on the mat. The woodpecker on the morning lawn. The phone call. The dinner with friends. The serious movie. The Cardiff City football game. The walk in the park. The chess game. The book. The poem. Moreover, didn't Camus contend that Sisyphus was an absurd hero, a man who had work to do, a happy man?

I ponder on Sisyphus's fate. Lonely, pushing up that boulder in all weathers – but sometimes pausing to observe perhaps errant sheep or a wild goat leaping from crag to crag. I see him climbing with his burden near drystone walls and an ancient hut, past sparse trees bent by the wind. How small he looks below the gaunt black cliffs! And reaching higher elevations, maybe he hesitates again near a lichen-clad rock to survey below a fathomless pool of water in a great pan of rocks. Above him, surely, curlews call and streams of liquid silver abseil down sides of granite slabs. A happy man then – or at least a sometimes happy man because of the majestic views, because of the rock-climbing strangers he may meet on the way, because of the work he has to do as he breathes in the sweet mountain air. And before sleep, look! Moonlight on the mountains.

February 6th
Slept late for a change. One of those grey days sterile with idleness. During the morning's slow grey inch of time reversing itself away from eternity I saw no one, thought nothing much, did nothing much.

Earlier this afternoon I went out to buy some cotton wool from Boots. When I returned I pressed the answer-phone button: YOU HAVE NO MESSAGE. I stood for a while by the front window hoping for something to happen in the street outside. A white van passed. Soon a nameless pedestrian with his head flexed, weighed down perhaps by the masculine London glooms of the featureless afternoon, walked up the slope from Dunstan Road. Nearby, the other side of our hedge, a car halted. The driver had difficulty in parking the vehicle. I felt abused by the pointlessness of it all.

I miss Joan so much. Then I noticed in our small front garden, amongst the overgrown grass, the surprised splash of yolk-yellow: the first February crocuses, herald of spring. Meanwhile my breath had misted a small patch of the window. I was about to touch the glass with my fingertip when a light came on like a secret signal in an upstairs room of the house opposite. I turned away to switch on the electric light here and to write this urban snapshot. The temperature has dropped with the smudge of evening. Outside, the cold is on the crocus.

Then

It must have been a quiet Sunday afternoon more than thirty years ago. Jeremy Robson had visited me and was about to leave. We were at the front gate when, startled, we saw down the otherwise deserted road a richly, brightly ribboned horse and cart coming towards us. As it came nearer we observed that the gaunt-looking driver was peculiarly dressed in a funereal satin-black outfit and wore a nineteenth-century tall black top hat. A batty cargo of coloured balloons, all filled with moon-air, bounced in the cart. As he passed, the driver did not acknowledge us, did not smile, certainly did not raise his hat. Soon he and his horse and cart disappeared and the clatter of its going ceased.

It could have been a vision from a waking dream, or a scene made for a film director such as Fellini. Mr Death dressed up for a carnival.

February 8th

Two preachers were featured on the TV news last night. Martin Luther King (thousands attended the funeral of his wife) and Abu Hamza, the radical Islamic cleric who has just been convicted at the Old Bailey on charges related to terrorism. What contrasting racial messages and calls to action these charismatics preached. Both possessed an extraordinary quality that gave them magical power over their audiences.

Psychoanalysts have pointed out how there remains a longing in all of us to discover a god-like personage with unlimited power and wisdom such as we thought our parents possessed when we were infants. Certainly the charismatic appeals to many by being imposing and authoritative and by giving orders in a paternal manner while, at the same time, offering disciples maternal caring and succour. I remember a lecture on 'Charisma, Anomie and the Psychopathic Personality' delivered by my psychoanalyst brother, Wilfred, where he compared charismatic leadership to the rapport of the hypnotist with his subject.

'The cardinal event in the rapport of hypnotist and subject,' Wilfred said, 'is the thorough occupation of the subject's mind by the hypnotist. This *engourdissement d'esprit* results in a restriction of consciousness, a selective, concentrated and expectant attention devoted to the hypnotist and his behaviour, and a simultaneous indifference to even massive excitations emanating from anyone else. The procedures for inducing hypnoses are basically appeals to *awe* and to *love*. In the first of these, matters of decisive importance are the social and professional prestige of the hypnotist, his imposing behaviour and his self-assurance in issuing commands. In the second, a mild and friendly attitude, a low monotonous voice and a restful atmosphere, including perhaps a darkened soundless room and soothing light stroking, are important ingredients. Sandor Ferenczi – Freud's distinguished pupil – discussed the connections of the first method with the child's conception of the firm, infallible, and all-powerful father, whereas the second or maternal method is redolent of scenes in which a mother woos her child to sleep by singing lullabies. The paternal and maternal inductions may be mixed. Appeals to awe and love especially characterise the efforts of charismatic leaders to fascinate their audiences and secure a following.' One may add here that Ferenczi went too far with therapeutic maternal experiences of love. Freud hearing that his pupil resorted to kissing his patients wrote a wonderfully acerbic letter (see Appendix Five).

The difference, of course, between Martin Luther King and Abu Hamza is marked. No one, balanced, would describe Luther King's charismatic rhetoric and gestures as sick whereas Abu Hamza is obviously half-insane and would inoculate his followers with his madness. But like most charismatic leaders both knew the force of words, both indeed had the gift of persuasive oratory, and both used the devices of rhetoric: linguistic ornaments, and rhythmic artifice.

We are suspicious of rhetoric, of demagoguery. We live in a thermonuclear era and have every reason to be fearful of destructive leadership. At the same time we have masses of despairing people who are looking for a saviour, and who could be infected by their master's contagious paranoia as happened in Hitler's Nazi Germany and elsewhere. Such bleak times we live in. We have to remind ourselves that rhetoric can also be a beneficial force. Martin Luther King proved it to be so. He would have agreed with Cicero, 'Tell me how many men would ever be able to bend their minds to the observation of uprightness and justice; how would they have consented to yield their wishes to those of their fellows; how would they have been persuaded to make a common cause of the common interest, and in their interest to sacrifice at need even their life, if it had not been by the aid and means of persuasion and eloquence and rhetoric?'

February 9th

I've been thinking more about rhetoric – how, irrespective of its message if that's possible, it can give us pleasure when it approaches, with its parallel ringing tones, the hypnotic power of poetry. Rhetoric propagates itself, loves repetition of sound and sense, proliferates ornament and generalisation where poetry is more economical and usually crystallises thought and feeling.

Yet there are many great examples of fine poetry, not only in the Bible, that are almost indistinguishable from rich rhetoric. Who speaks, for example, these lines, a poet or an orator?

Not a grave of the murder'd for freedom but grows
    seed for freedom, in its turn to bear seed,
Which the winds carry afar and resow, and the rains
    and the showers nourish.
Not a disembodied spirit can the weapon of tyrants
    let loose
But it stalks invisibly over the earth, whispering,
    counselling, cautioning.
Liberty, let others despair of you – I never despair you.
Is the house shut? Is the master away?
Nevertheless, be ready, be not weary of watching,
He will soon return, his messengers come anon.

These lines are recognisably by a poet. In fact, by Walt
Whitman, yet they break all the rules. They tend to
generalise as oratory does; they own the same hypnotic
power as oratory does; they lean on abstract rhetorical
words like 'liberty'; they do not crystallise.

February 10th
When it comes to listening to music, say to a Beethoven
quartet, I do not have a long concentration span. Too
often thoughts arrive, do not conjugate with the music
but rove truantly, and muffle it. After an hiatus of not
listening I become conscious of the music again and
try consciously to re-surrender to the music's progres-
sive enchantment.

    It happened last night when I switched on the radio
and listened to Elgar's elegiac Cello Concerto.
Jacqueline du Pré. At one point I began thinking of
my unsuccessful visit to her house in Knightsbridge.

Jacqueline du Pré had converted to Judaism on marrying
Daniel Barenboim and her rabbi, Albert Friedlander,
a man I liked and respected, had telephoned me. 'You
know Jacqueline suffers from MS and doesn't perform
any longer. She expressed a desire to hear you read
some of your poems to her. It would be a mitzvah.
Will you come to Rutland Gate Gardens where she
lives?'

It would be a privilege to do so. I wondered what
poems to choose. I have written several poems
about music, one being a series of definitions of music
in sonnet form – rather like George Herbert who
had offered definitions in fourteen lines of prayer.
I had called my sonnet, with great originality,
'Music'.

When I arrived at Rutland Gate Gardens I felt rather
like Felix Mendelssohn visiting Queen Victoria at
Buckingham Palace. Albert was there (not the Prince
Consort) and he quietly introduced me to Jacqueline
du Pré and her companion. Eventually I began my
reading of the sonnet, 'Music':

Music in the beginning, before the Word,
    voyaging of the spheres, their falling transport.
Like phoenix utterance, what Pythagoras heard;
    first hallucinogen, ritual's afterthought.

A place on no map. Hubbub behind high walls
    of Heaven – its bugged secrets filtering out:
numinous hauntings; sacerdotal mating-calls;
    decorous deliriums; an angel's shout.

If God's propaganda, then Devil's disgust,
  plainchant or symphony, carol or fugue;
King Saul's solace, St Cecilia's drug;
  silence's hiding-place — like sunbeams' dust.

Sorrow's aggrandisements more plangent than sweet;
  the soul made audible, Time's other beat.

As I read the poem I realised Jacqueline du Pré fidgeted
and was not attentive. After a second poem I gave up.
She clutched at a piece of paper and it was evident she
wished to read her verse to me. So I became her auditor
and was not a little disconcerted by the barrack-room
filth of the limericks she recited. I think I might have
been more shocked than Rabbi Friedlander. I did not
expect it from her. Her limerick vulgarity would have
outclassed a first-year Saturday-night medical student.

I left Rutland Gate Gardens somewhat diminished.
I had come to read poetry and having failed to do so
my pride I suppose was bruised. Only later did I allow
myself to empathise with Jacqueline du Pré's tragic
predicament. The playing of the cello had been her real
life. She, a hugely talented volatile musician, would have
become her most pure extraordinary self while she
played. And now her neurological condition would not
permit it. There are testaments by musicians and
composers who through disease became partly exiled
from themselves. Beethoven continued to compose after
he was deaf. Even so, what is more poignant than his
Heiligenstadt Testament, which he addressed to his
brothers Karl and Johann? (See Appendix Six.) If

Jacqueline du Pré had a literary gift equal to her musical one she would have penned no ineffectual limericks but told her plangent story of a paradise lost that we, her admirers, would never forget.

February 11th
The Cardiff City FC fanzine dropped through the letter box this morning. My son, David, writes a column for it and generally makes witty remarks. But on this occasion he was outdone by Gordon Strachan, the football manager. When asked by a reporter, 'Gordon, can we have a quick word please?' Strachan replied, 'Velocity,' and walked away.

I toyed with the idea of visiting Cardiff for the day to watch the Bluebirds play Stoke. After all I possess a season ticket and have missed so many matches this season. In the past, frequently, during home fixtures we would be staying at Ogmore so off I would go the twenty-three miles to Ninian Park while Joan selflessly stayed behind to garden before shutting up shop. We usually returned to London on a Saturday night. I would catch the 5.25 p.m. train from Cardiff Central. Joan, meanwhile, had caught the same train earlier at Bridgend and would keep a seat for me in Carriage D as arranged.

But the moping thought of returning from Cardiff in that carriage, or any other, without Joan, and then trekking via Paddington back to our house here in Golders Green — the rooms dark, February-cold, unwelcoming — made me hesitate. Languorous, indecisive, by 11 a.m. I gave up the idea altogether. Besides, it was already too late.

Instead, this afternoon I listened to the Radio Wales commentary of the game via the technical miracle of digital TV. The commentary was frustrating. I wanted to know what was happening on the pitch but I had to endure chatter about past players, the nostalgia of past games, boring statistics, the irrelevant scores at the venues of other current matches. In the atrophied background I could hear the crowd signal drama by ooing and aahing and by punctuated loud boos, which, in translation, meant that the referee had been bribed by the Stoke management. As those who sit near me in the Stand always point out the ref is English, at least never Welsh!

Steve who occupies the next seat to mine is fundamentally religious – so much so that his linguistic aggression towards the referee is invariably filtered through a vocabulary sieve, to become, at worst, 'Flippin' 'eck.' I missed hearing his flipping 'ecks, I missed that other season-ticket holder who once shouted out, 'Fuckin' ungentlemanly be'aviour.' I even missed the raucous, too-loud tannoy's preliminary music such as the martial 'Men of Harlech' and the hysterical shouting voice just before the game begins, 'SUPPORT THE BOYS ... MAKE ... SOME ... NOISE.' Most of all I missed watching the game, but the radio commentary was better than nothing, especially as Cardiff won 3–0.

Then
Three years ago my cousin, Richard Shepherd, himself a radio sports commentator who edits the Cardiff City

Saturday programme, arranged for me to be interviewed by Mark Aizlewood at a Cardiff City FC Supporters Function along with Ian Rush the Welsh ex-international. Alas, snowfall prevented Ian Rush from travelling down from North Wales. Halfway through the interview I was asked whether I would like to be a football commentator like Richard. I replied truthfully, 'No. It would be a distraction – rather like reading a book about sex technique while one was trying to enjoy sexual intercourse.' The two hundred or so threateningly silent faces who no doubt for the most part were wondering who the hell I was, and why a poet was being interviewed, suddenly burst out wildly cheering. It was one of my finest moments. I wished Gordon Strachan had been there.

February 14th

When my mother was ageing and living alone in her Cathedral Road flat in Cardiff she used to say, 'I often keep the wireless on for company.' Sunday evening I realised I was doing exactly that. I reread the invitation to celebrate the publication of a Russian poetry anthology edited by my friends, Daniel Weissbort and his Russian wife, Valentina, at Joseph's Bookshop Café in Finchley Road – only one mile away. I switched off the radio.

At the welcoming café I sat at a table with Anthony Rudolf and Moris Farhi who both knew Joan. When Tony Rudolf asked me how I was managing I should have responded with one of my stock simple answers – 'I'm OK' or 'I'm coping, thank you'. Instead I told him the truth, 'not very well' and seeing him wince I realised I had discomforted him needlessly.

As I listened to Susannah York, Ruth Fainlight and Elaine Feinstein reading versions of Russian poems I recalled yet again Robert Frost's, 'Poetry is that which is lost in translation'. There are a number of foreign language poems magically transformed into English into which one can go sober and leave a little drunk. But Frost is generally right, especially these days when so many translator-poets are monolingual. At best so often what the reader is being offered is creative plagiarism. I plead guilty to it myself, though I can't imagine say, Christopher Marlowe translating Ovid if he had not known Latin. Different times, different mores.

My own poems have been translated into languages I cannot understand, Italian, Polish, Czech, etc. and though I am happy enough to boast about it, I'm not overwhelmed by the honour. I'm curious to know how much these veiled versions resemble the originals, but that's about all. A coincidence. Stop ... I was about to ...

A few minutes ago (it is just past ten o'clock) the post heavily dropped on the hall doormat. One envelope including an official form from my Polish publisher! The form was bilingual. Beneath the Polish I read: *Information on Revenue (Income) derived by non-resident natural person.* Being strangely called a 'natural person' reminded me of how poetry is mistranslated. T. S. Eliot's 'Journey of the Magi' which begins 'A cold coming we had of it/ Just the worst time of the year/ For a journey/ ...'

has been bungled into German as 'We had a cold coming/ Just the worst time for a journey . . .'

Paul Zimmer, the American poet related to me his experience of being translated into Japanese. He had dedicated his book to his wife: *To Sue, with love* adorned the flyleaf. When a copy of the translations arrived he learnt from a Japanese friend the dedication now read: *To bring a lawsuit with love.*

I enjoyed my night out at Joseph's Book Store Café though I guessed that sometimes the musical exuber-ance of the Russian poems had invariably been flat-tened, and that which had originally been pungent, in English became faint.

Back in the silence of the house in Golders Green, I turned on the radio.

Then

Scores of poets from different countries used to be invited to the annual International Poetry Festival at Struga, Macedonia. One of these poems would be translated into Macedonian. The original poem used to be read by the poet followed by an actor reciting the Macedonian version. The Poetry Readings would take place in various venues in Ochra, Skopje, and elsewhere. This meant, of course, that the poets heard the same selected poems several times.

The first year the British Council sent me there the Macedonians chose my poem 'Hunt the Thimble' to be translated – all two pages of it. The problem was that after the first two readings the actor mislaid one of the pages. So, after my reading of 'Hunt the Thimble', the

Macedonian mutation seemed amazingly brief. When I returned from the microphone to my platform seat next to Seamus Heaney he whispered to me in his ripe Irish accent, 'Ach, sure, Dannie, now I know poetry is that which is lost in translation.'

February 15th
So, at last, the MPs in a free vote have sensibly passed a bill that will prevent people smoking in pubs, restaurants, clubs, etc. About time, since substances other than nicotine in cigarette smoke – the polynuclear hydrocarbons and radioactive isotopes of polonium – are carcinogenic. At one time, and not so long ago, even arsenic could have been inhaled by a cigarette smoker until those who manage the tobacco plantations restricted the use of arsenical insecticides.

Strange to think that in the sixteenth century tobacco was considered to be a cure-all. Its leaves were applied to wounds and its smoke blown up the rectum. But some were wary of the weed. Ben Jonson sighed, 'Ods me, I marvel what pleasure or felicity they have in taking their roguish tobacco. It's good for nothing but to choke a man, and fill him full of smoke and embers.'

Tobacco smoking is an addiction rather than a bad habit. For decades I worked in a chest clinic and would see the shadows of death-warrants on the X-rays of cigarette smokers; yet I was forty-six years of age before I managed to overcome my tobacco needs. In the clinic, for too long, I had to say to patients, 'Don't do as I do, do as I tell you.'

Then

The most eccentric shop keeper I ever encountered was a tobacconist. He took pleasure in startling and teasing his potential customers. 'Senior Service you want?' he'd say. 'I've run out of them. You can have twenty Capstan if you like.' Or 'Twenty Goldflake? Sorry, sir, they only make them in hundreds.'

His small shop in Cleveland Street across the road from the Middlesex Hospital was itself remarkable for its shabbiness. It must have been in the early 1950s that I first entered it. That occasion, there was no sign of the tobacconist. Behind a worm-eaten, decrepit, stained counter, stacks of shelves carrying huge dummy cartons climbed up the wall, leaving space for a dusty, cracked glass case, the shelves of which were empty. I remember coughing and shuffling on the bare floor-boards hoping that the proprietor of the shop would hear me.

At last, from behind a plywood partition a small elderly kyphotic man appeared. He wore a trilby hat much too large for him so that its brim settled horizontally low over his forehead. (On later visits, he wore the same hat – it seemed he hardly ever discarded it.) Before I could speak he complained how much it cost him to feed his dog, which he had just finished feeding, but he affirmed, 'A living do-og is better than a dead lion.' I'm sure I must have bashfully smiled and nodded before asking for twenty Players. He ignored my request but continued his soliloquy about dogs especially those that had become proverbial: Argus, Beautiful Joe, Jip Katmir, Rin Tin Tin. His long monologue was interrupted when a woman entered the shop. She seemed to be in a hurry and impatiently asked for ten Craven A. The old tobacconist told her that she would have to go to Paraguay to buy Craven A – and addressing me added that he had a relative in Villarrica, in Paraguay, who never wrote to him! The woman, evidently feeling snubbed, made some wordless noise before turning to quit the shop.

The old tobacconist with a quizzical expression on his face shrugged his shoulders and muttered about women smoking and what a disgrace it was. In his day, he informed me, 'No respectable woman smoked.' It must have been five minutes later before I left the shop triumphantly clutching a packet of twenty Players.

February 17th
I spoke to Dr Meehan on the phone. He has made an appointment for me to see him next Wednesday. He has a pleasant Irish accent that resembles that of the psychiatrist who used to preside during the radio programme, 'In the Psychiatrist's Chair'. I don't relish ventilating my feelings in his consulting room as I'm expected to. The fact is that though most of the time I cope and must appear balanced to strangers, every now and then, without Joan pointing direction I feel I'm lost in a foreign city and have to stop to read myself as if I were a map.

February 18th
I keep thinking about my appointment with Dr Meehan next Wednesday and how, inevitably, I shall have to

speak of Joan. I fear that I might then be womanly, like Niobe, all tears. I know I shouldn't feel any shame about crying in front of another person. But 'Big Boys Don't Cry' has been stencilled into my very being as it has into the natures of most men born and brought up in Britain.

Before the accident last June, over all the past decades, I can't recall hardly ever being brought to unbidden tears. Now I'm a veritable onion, a storehouse of tears. And all the time and everywhere there are the thistles of remembrance. Strange how some things have become more meaningful. Not only events in the great world, public or personal, but certain past memories and fictional texts. Even certain poems that I seem to have known all my life. How often have I, as a boy and as an adult, heard Wilfred quote his favourite lines – Tennyson's 'Tears, idle tears ...' Now when I read the poem I respond to it as if I have read it for the first time.

Tears, idle tears, I know not what they mean,
Tears from the depth of some divine despair
Rise in the heart, and gather to the eyes,
In looking on the happy autumn-fields,
And thinking of the days that are no more.

Fresh as the first beam glittering on a sail,
That brings our friends up from the underworld,
Sad as the last which reddens over one
That sinks with all we love below the verge;
So sad, so fresh, the days that are no more.

Ah, sad and strange as in dark summer dawns
The earliest pipe of half-awaken'd birds
To dying ears, when unto dying eyes
The casement slowly grows a glimmering square;
So sad, so strange, the days that are no more.

Dear as remember'd kisses after death,
And sweet as those by hopeless fancy feign'd
On lips that are for others; deep as love,
Deep as first love, and wild with all regret;
O Death in Life, the days that are no more.

February 19th

Woke up too early again. Another upsetting dream: I was angry with my wife because she wanted a divorce. But the shadowy figure I raged at did not have distinct features, certainly not those of Joan. That's one dream for this Daniel to interpret, I think, rather than the psychiatrist next Wednesday.

Over breakfast I read the newspaper account about the presumably forlorn 520 inmates at Guantan*amo* Bay prison who may or may not be potential terrorists. Amo means 'I love', doesn't it? Tony Blair calls that barbed electrified-wire compound an anomaly. I would call it, as others would, a concentration camp. Blair's semantic detoxica-tion reminds me of Amir Gilboa's comment about how politicians sweeten the semantically unpalatable:

They shed a man's blood.
I said Blood.
Smiling, they said Paint.

Our echoing, heartless Victorian-old jails here are nothing to be proud of. I gather those in the USA are worse, and not a few resonate with only partially repressed brutality. They are, like Guantanamo Bay in Cuba, a contradiction to the nation's most significant icon, the Statue of Liberty. I first saw that gigantic statue from a low-flying aeroplane in 1966, the time of the Vietnam War. The statue was the same colour as that of the dollar bill. I recall staring from the window seat of a turbo-prop plane that had just left New York's LaGuardia airport for Washington. I saw the shadow of the aeroplane shaped like a cross on the water below. It moved horizontally, nearer and nearer to the Statue of Liberty before finally crucifying it.

February 20th

I have too many books. When another one, unsolicited, thuds on the mat below the letter box the bookshelves all over the house groan. This morning's slim volume (not so slim) is by an American poet.

I should like to cull many of my books, especially those in the extensive poetry shelves, yet I hesitate to do so. Too many of those that I would take to the Oxfam shop are signed by the author, by one I do not or hardly know. Moreover, they usually have a brief warm inscription in the title page or flyleaf: *To Dannie Abse*, etc. Difficult. Other books of course I'm glad to own and am pleased that they have been signed by a 'Colleague in the Art'. One signature that would baffle a book collector is to be found on the title page of my own *Collected Poems: 1948–1976*. It is that of John Betjeman and is there by accident.

Then

I understood from the phone call that London Weekend Television hoped to broadcast a series of seven programmes entitled, *John Betjeman and Friends*. First, though, they wanted to make a pilot and I was invited to be John Betjeman's friend though, in fact, we had never met. The pilot programme was set for April 12th 1977 and Prunella Scales would be there also to read some poetry chosen by Betjeman.

That April day I had lunch with Betjeman before we went into the studio to face the cameras and a muted audience. 'The first poem I've chosen,' said Betjeman, 'is Thomas Hood's "I Remember, I Remember the house where I was born". Some may think it sentimental but it isn't, it isn't, and I don't care if it is.' He then, staring straight ahead, chanted those extraordinary lines that I had carelessly thought twee. As I listened to his intense recitation I realised how the rhythm of the poem had lulled and half-disguised its extreme pathos. Its depressive tones reminded me how Thomas Hood had continually suffered physical ill health and had had chronic pecuniary problems which his wife and children knew only too well. It so happened – a coincidence – that only the previous week I had read a long daft poem of Hood's called, 'Miss Kilmansegg and Her Precious Leg' and asked John Betjeman if he knew it.

John Betjeman gasped, opened his eyes wide. I thought
he was going to rise from his chair. 'How very good of
you to know that poem,' he cried out delightedly, as if
I had given him some valuable gift. 'Oh thank you,
thank you very much, Dannie.' He was being sincere I
realised, not pulling *my* valuable leg. He continued to
speak rhapsodically about the merits of Hood's verse
and his proclivity to write puns in them. Indeed, Thomas
Hood's dying words are supposed to be a pun uttered
to his wife, 'My dear, oh my dear, you are losing your
lively hood!'

'I'm going to read Edward Thomas's "Adlestrop" this
afternoon,' said John Betjeman. 'Afterwards perhaps
you'll read your "Not Adlestrop". But first we'll discuss
Edward Thomas's true talent. Does that suit you?'

While we sampled lunch I realised how ephemeral
was John Betjeman's rhapsodic mood. He was towards
the end of his life and an invalid. He had to be pushed
in a wheelchair to the studio and I wondered whether
these TV programmes would be his last.

At the rehearsal he occasionally would become befud-
dled. The producer of the programme was worried
though not Prunella Scales. She whispered to me 'I've
worked with Sir John a number of times. He bumbles
along at rehearsal but he'll be all right when it comes
to the real thing.'

Alas, the real thing in front of a patient audience
only stuttered along because of Betjeman's blanks of
forgetfulness. At one point I had to prompt him, 'And
you particularly like Edward Thomas's "Adlestrop",'

I said. He smiled and that innocent look of rhapsodic pleasure again inhabited his face as he recited,

> Yes, I remember Adlestrop —
> The name, because one afternoon
> Of heat the express-train drew up there.
> Unwontedly. It was late June.
>
> The steam hissed. Someone cleared his throat.
> No one left and no one came
> On the bare platform. What I saw
> Was Adlestrop — only the name
>
> And willow, willow-herb, and grass,
> And meadowsweet, and haycocks dry,
> No whit less still and lonely fair
> Than the high cloudlets in the sky.
>
> And for that minute a blackbird sang
> Close by, and round him, mistier,
> Farther and farther, all the birds
> Of Oxfordshire and Gloucestershire.

Afterwards we discussed the merits of the poem, the way it begins conversationally and other details such as 'someone cleared his throat' which economically evokes the silence that surrounded the small railway station's platform. But our dialogue was too prolonged. I was waiting for him to invite me to read 'Not Adlestrop' as planned. Finally I had to say, 'I think you wanted me to contrast Adlestrop with —'

'Ah yes. You've written a not Adlestrop poem. Do
read it. *Do.*'

Not Adlestrop, no — besides, the name
hardly matters. Nor did I languish in June heat.
Simply, I stood, too early, on the empty platform,
and the wrong train came in slowly, surprised,
    stopped.
Directly facing me, from a window,
a very, *very* pretty girl leaned out.

    When I, all instinct,
stared at her, she, all instinct, inclined her head away
as if she'd divined the much married life in me,
or as if she might spot, up platform,
some unlikely familiar.

For my part, under the clock, I continued
my scrutiny with unmitigated pleasure.
And she knew it, she certainly knew it, and would
    not
glance at me in the silence of not Adlestrop.

    Only when the train heaved noisily, only
when it jolted, when it slid away, only *then,*
daring and secure, she smiled back at my smile,
and I, daring and secure, waved back at her waving.

And so it was, all the way down the hurrying
    platform
as the train gathered atrocious speed
towards Oxfordshire or Gloucestershire.

The programme over it was evident that many in the audience had brought John Betjeman's books with them. They soon surrounded the table at which we sat and held out their books for signature. The TV producer beckoned me to one side.

'I'm afraid we won't go on with the series,' he said. 'Sir John's no longer up to it. It's sad.'

When I returned to the table to pick up my *Collected Poems* from which I read 'Not Adlestrop' I saw that Betjeman had signed it unintentionally with all the other books thrust towards him.

February 21st

I'm somewhat fearful at the prospect of sitting opposite a certain Dr John Meehan, a consultant psychiatrist at the Chelsea and Westminster Hospital, but tomorrow I shall have to do so. I shall be, unusually, the other side of the counter and will need to talk about the accident since Dr Meehan, for legal reasons, has to report the extent of my 'post-traumatic stress' and, presumably, will need to know its provenances. I shall have to relive, with difficulty, those moments in the car on the night of June 13th when I slowed down to less than 50 mph as I prepared to quit the motorway for the slip road that would have taken us to Ogmore via Bridgend.

As I write now too close to tears, I hear the gigantic crash from the rear before our car capsizes and I shout soon afterwards, 'Are you all right, Joan?' I receive no answer. Over the last eight months occasions such as an ambulance's siren screaming have led to flashbacks where I am escaping from the prison of the car. Later, nameless people including a woman who declared she had been a nurse, and a fireman, try to attend me while I keep reassuring them that I'm all right, that I'm a doctor and know that I'm OK. Meanwhile I see Joan's face pale beneath the darkness of all that upturned chaos of tortuous metal. Someone is trying to put a brace on my neck and a woman, a young woman whom I assume to be the driver of the other lethal car is running up and down the verge of the M4 hysterically sobbing 'I'm sorry, I'm sorry, I'm sorry'. (Had she been asleep while driving?)

I do not know Joan has been killed instantly, I do not know why my face and neck are cut and bleeding. I do not even know I have several fractured ribs. I know only that Joan is only yards away, inert, and that I am struggling with the solicitous fireman; that I'm trying to be free of his tight clasp, until finally enraged, powerless, I yell at him, 'Fuck off.' He replies with genteel, incongruous propriety, 'There's no need to swear, doctor.' Then I ask the woman who said she had been a nurse to please take Joan's pulse. In the darkness I am only vaguely aware of the sibilant reiteration of occasional traffic passing by. The ex-nurse returns from the mangled car and tells me, 'Your wife has no pulse.'

The ambulance arrives. The fireman strangely whispers to me, 'I'll do anything you want for you. Anything at all. I'll visit you at the hospital.' (He did.) Soon I am in the ambulance on my way to the Prince of Wales Hospital in Bridgend. Someone is taking my pulse.

February 24th

Dr Meehan is a comfortably built Irishman with a seemingly amiable and sympathetic disposition. As I expected
I went into his consulting room with a dry handker-
chief and left with a somewhat damp one. He told me
what I know: that I am experiencing the combined
symptoms of bereavement ('what's gone and what's past
help is not past grief') and those of post-traumatic
stress (flashbacks to the scene of the accident, reluc-
tance to drive a car especially at night, anomie when I
enter surroundings new to me, etc.).

What can I say to him other than that for me there
is no music in the nightingale without Joan. He is an
Irishman. I should have quoted Yeats:

> All that's beautiful drifts away
> Like the waters

February 28th

I received an interesting letter on Friday from a friend
of mine who years ago worked for the publisher, J. M.
Dent and Sons. She enclosed a reader's report on the
submitted manuscript of Dylan Thomas's *Under Milk
Wood*. My friend relates how she was tidying up old
papers at her home when she came across the report
which was by Desmond McCarthy, a leading literary
reviewer for the *Sunday Times*. His report for Dent was
dated two days before Dylan died in America and is
one long rant and sneer. Surprising, really, because as
far as I can remember Desmond McCarthy was not in

the habit of handing rough thistles to the author he was reviewing.

He acknowledged Dylan Thomas's verbal felicity but this gift of his he reckoned 'is consistently debased throughout the play to portray the crude, the vulgar, the irreverent and the obscene . . . Its dominant theme makes the work literally a prostitution of poetic art . . . Not since the days of his fellow Welshman, Caradoc Evans, has Wales suffered such brutal treatment at the hands of one of her own sons!' The long report concludes, 'The fact that this play is to be broadcast by the BBC is a very sorry commentary on the type of culture that the licence holder gets for his money!' Dent, of course, went ahead and published it despite McCarthy's strictures.

It's not just the odd English critic who would disparagingly ask, 'Hath not thy rose a canker, Dylan?' A section of the Welsh literary elite by critical text and by word of mouth over the decades has heated up the furnace of negative criticism, especially about *Under Milk Wood*. They diminish it by categorising it as a mere entertainment lacking ambition, and clamour that it is a false portrait of a Welsh community. Dylan, himself gave these critics ammunition when he frivolously called his play for voices *Llarregub* (Bugger all). And it's true that it is a cartoon. Cartoons, though, do have their intrinsic truths. Ask Dickens. Ask even Kafka. Besides I swear by St David and all the fish in Bala Lake that there are more cartoon personalities in Wales than eccentrics in England. And what's wrong with that?

Then

I'm thinking of a number of Welsh cartoon figures I have known who could live happily in *Under Milk Wood* — most of all perhaps Dr Ernie Lloyd who worked as a consultant physician at Westminster Hospital while I was a medical student. When I attended his lectures I thought how in looks and in sheer stature he resembled Lloyd George — who once remarked, by the way, that in Wales we measure people from the neck up.

Ernie would, with his right hand, brush back his over-long white-grey Lloyd George hair as he stood at the lectern and stare at us piercingly until we, on the rising benches before him, settled our whisperings and fidgetings and shufflings. At the very first lecture of his I attended (on the cardiovascular system) he suddenly flung out his arms horizontally as if he'd been nailed to a cross and in a lilting accented voice he drawled, 'The ... old ... 'eart.' After a meaningful pause, with histrionic gestures, he continued. 'The old 'eart beats seventy, duw, eighty times a minute. Systole, diastole. Minute in, minute out. Hour in, hour out. Day in, day out. Systole, diastole. Week in, week out. Year in, year out ... The old 'eart.' He had moved his hands like a conductor to accompany that incantation. Now he lowered his voice as if he was telling us some prurient secret. 'Do you know, boys, what the sound of a mitral murmur resembles? It's like ... it's like the wind gently rustlin' through the corn.' He stopped his peroration seemingly to appreciate the simile he had just uttered. He then supplied the commentary: 'Poetic, isn't it, boys?'

Yes, Ernie Lloyd could have been a doctor in *Under Milk Wood*.

March 1st

St David's Day and still the unrelenting winter weather. Late this mind-numbing morning I decided to brave the depressing weather of Golders Green Road and possibly, just possibly, buy myself some warm trousers. The thick grey ageing Marks and Spencer ones I've been wearing have been enjoyed by a wayward moth. Already, last winter, Joan had urged me to discard them. 'Get a new pair for heaven's sake,' she had pleaded. 'You could pass those on to your brother.'

That was a family joke. She was referring back to the 1960s when my brother, Leo, then a member of parliament, and forever a dandy would play the fool and dress up — outrageous tall top hat, ostentatious coloured waistcoat etc. — each Budget Day. I, irritated by gleeful strangers remarking on his sartorial exotic exhibitionism, would respond invariably with a grave, 'Yes, Leo wears my cast-offs.' Privately, I disapproved of Leo's prancing in Parliament. He would mock me. 'You're too much worried about what the neighbours will say,' he laughed. But I recalled how Herbert Spenser writing about Manners and Fashion had quoted, 'If you show yourself eccentric in matters of dress, the world will not listen to you ... The opinions you express on important subjects, which might have been treated with respect ... will now be put down among your singularities, and thus by dissenting in trifles, you disable yourself from spreading dissent in essentials.' It was OK for a poet such as myself to dress carelessly but not a serious reforming politician. Or so I argued then.

When I entered a clothes shop in Golders Green Road I was immediately greeted with excessive diligence by an assistant who owned a surprising (assumed?) hoity-toity accent. 'Yars, can I help you, sar?' Wishing that he would not be so eager, I hesitated. 'I'm looking for some thick wool trousers,' I said at last. He stared at me as if I had made a shameful confession. 'Oh no, sar,' he said superiorly. 'Thick wool trousers? Oh no no no sar. They don't make them nowadays. People live in centrally heated houses and have cars.' He stood up straight in noble eminence and clutched with each hand the two lapels of his smart blue suit.

'People go out, if only to walk to their cars,' I objected.

I sensed he disapproved of me. He eventually discerned I was not interested, as he was, in fashion. Nevertheless I began to wish I had dressed up a bit before entering his emporium and not revealed that I was one who belonged to that class who cling to worn clothes and to what is comfortable.

Suddenly he released his hands from his lapels and, inspired, told me, 'Corduroy trousers, sar. Yars, we do have corduroy trousers. They keep out the cold wind though they're only cotton, you know.'

Joan, if not Leo, would surely have approved of the corduroy trousers I am wearing this afternoon as I write this inconsequential note. The world wags. Here, now, I think of Joan. I think of the colours in the clothes *she* favoured. I try not to think of Joan. Difficult. All around and about me in this room I see evidence of things she chose or placed there and there: the paintings on the walls; the objects on the windowsill, that unusual vase she brought back from Mexico.

For a silly moment I long to be in the Land of Elsewhere where there is no swan that is solitary and no little red worm – a fraudulent place but beautiful like Yeats's Lake Isle or Cézanne's perfect apples.

Here, when will the cold leave the crocus and cease to be a guest in this house?

March 2nd

This morning I came across a card Joan must have bought when we visited the Victoria Art Gallery in Bath. It's a portrait of 'Old Tom Thumb' by Thomas Barker (1769–1847). Perhaps Joan kept it as a memento because she admired it or possibly because I might have droned on about Old Tom Thumb's medical condition!

We think of Tom Thumb as a midget. But the portrait by Thomas Barker suggests a clinical picture of acromegaly, a condition where pituitary growth hormones have been overactive, leading to gigantism and overgrowth of the nose, the jaw etc. Perhaps Barker's model had been a giant not a dwarf and his designation 'Old Tom Thumb' an ironic nickname. Just as tall people are sometimes called 'Tiny'. Joan would gently mock me for being so medically eyed.

Of course it's not always possible to escape from the education of one's impressionable years. In art galleries, on occasions, I have discovered that my medical training can interfere with my purely aesthetic appreciation of a portrait. In the National Portrait Gallery, I have diagnosed jaundice (probably haemolytic), acne, rosacea, profound anaemia, polycythaemia, thyrotoxicosis, and post-coital depression!

Now I venture to scrutinise Old Tom's features again. Thumb's right eyebrow is raised quizzically and the lips of his mouth a mere line because they are being pulled together, perhaps clenched in agitated frustrated wrath. His face is indeed a veritable battlefield of emotions. So what was Thomas Barker trying to express in this portrait? What thoughts raced from his brush to the canvas? Surely more than Tom Thumb's repressed rage at having to suffer the attendant symptoms of acromegaly. True art is a mystery, its deepest X can hardly be seen, never mind known. So I remind myself of the Talmud's command, 'Accustom thy tongue to say, "I know not".'

March 4th

The sun, unobstructed by any clouds, had springtime health though the keen wind was still winter-arctic as I walked through Golders Hill Park accompanied by the American doctor-poet Nobert Hirschorn and Elaine Feinstein. The snowdrops were still in evidence but the daffodils slept in their closed stagnation not yet ready to unfurl their silent trumpets and announce their fanfare for spring.

It seemed to me ironic that daffodils were my mother's

favourite flowers for they contain galanthamine which alkaloid is now used in the treatment of what my mother suffered in her old age – Alzheimer's disease. Apparently, tests have shown that if Wales's national flower is grown high up in the Black Mountains they yield more galanthamine than those daffodils which thrive near sea-level in Pembrokeshire. There is already talk in Wales of growing fields of daffodils in the uplands for, at present, the synthetic version of the drug is very expensive.

At the totally frozen pond near the flower garden the sleeping daffodils make me think of St David again, and how he used to stand up to his neck in the cold water of a lake or pond to recite the scriptures. I had a fleeting vision of him standing here, on the ice of the pond in Golders Hill Park, waving his thin bare arms. I blinked. His eidetic image faded as Elaine responded to Burt's question, 'Did you know Sylvia?'

At the top of the park is a wooden-planked restaurant. We sat there outdoors, on its verandah, drinking coffee, sheltered from the callous wind, enjoying the weak dilutions of liquid sunlight and the vain inconsequentiality of our literary talk and gossip of who loses and who wins, who's in, who's out.

March 7th

An advance copy of *Running Late* has arrived. Tony Whittome has ensured that it is a handsome production. It will probably be my last *new* book of poems, a coda to my *New and Collected* which appeared in 2003. Usually when I've had a new volume published I've been smugly sure and proud of its contents. (That was so with even my first two horribly flawed books of verse.) I feel less certain about the contents of *Running Late* — and that's not just because Joan isn't around to impatiently reassure me. The poems in the second half of the book are so personal and the specific gravity of emotion in the poems somehow altered because of what happened to Joan after I'd given in the book to Hutchinson. I suppose one stanza of a poem with the deliberately ambiguous title of 'Standing Still' confesses my uncertainties:

> Now reaching the last outpost of Pretend
> you see a reflection in the same window,
> a ghostly imitation of yourself,
> and ask, Do you still have four aces
> in your hand and the joker up your sleeve?
> So much rodomontade! And who's deceived?
> Is your song a frog's croak? Was your eagle
> a ladybird, your furnace a candle flame,
> your jewel a waterdrop on a grass blade?

Well I suppose a waterdrop on a grass blade is a beautiful thing. Anyway, the poems in the book that I shall in future years judge as successful or not at least attest to the transfiguration of something clarified that I have felt and thought, of something I have read or imperatively experienced told as narrative and sung as song. If now I'm blocked from composing further poems it is because I could only write in death's blank ink the same lament over and over.

March 10th

Over lunch yesterday my literary agent at PFD, Robert Kirby, was curious to know what I'm writing so, after hesitations, I've agreed to pass on to him the first fifty pages or so of this vulnerable manuscript. I have told him how I've listened to the small interior voice that keeps urging me, 'Physician, heal thyself', and that, as a result, I'm committed to this journal, this on-going prescription for self-regeneration. Robert asked me if this journal would be therapeutic or at least meaningful for others who have suffered a bereavement at one time or another.

What can I say? Different people adjust to an irrevocable fathomless loss presumably in similar ways and maybe there are those who by learning that this is so, by seeing another's barely disguised despair may feel a momentary consolation, feel a little less alone. I don't know.

March 11th

This morning the *Ham and High* sent John Horder here to interview me about my forthcoming *Running Late*. Tactful Horder may have been, but I found it difficult to talk about the love poems that conclude the book most of which directly addressed Joan when she was alive. Now, alas, the tense is wrong.

March 12th

Through Pat Wain I've learnt more about Old Tom Thumb whom Thomas Barker painted in 1789. He was nicknamed Tom Thumb not because of his height, as I had surmised, but because he sold miniature story books for children. He had a prodigiously long life of 110 years, married four times and fathered thirty-two children. So presumably he did not suffer from acromegaly since those pituitary giants usually lack a surfeit of sex hormones and have shortened lives because of other associated conditions such as diabetes. Despite Oliver Wendell Holmes's suggestion that the key to longevity is to suffer an incurable chronic disease and to coddle oneself carefully because of it, I know my spot diagnosis of acromegaly is wrong.

I can think of more memorable errors doctors have made. One concerns a much respected New York physician who, in the early twentieth century, could detect typhoid fever simply by palpating a symptomless person's tongue. This fantastic diagnostician would move through the ward, from bed to bed, while patients thrust out their tongues for him to feel. Though this or that patient had no early sign of typhoid the New York doctor would sadly pronounce, 'Your tongue, by its very texture, tells me you have contracted the salmonella typhi germs.'

Sure enough, the patient would eventually exhibit the symptoms of the disease – headache, lassitude, fever, bleeding from the nose, diarrhoea, etc. The doctor was proved right in an amazing number of cases. Only later was it discovered that he, himself, was a typhoid carrier and so had infected his patients through his tongue palpations.

March 14th

Woke up this morning an hour ago, pining for Joan and not ready to face the day. Nine months have passed and all manner of things don't get any easier. I hear the black dog barking in the near distance and turn for help by writing these pages. No news yet of when the coroner has fixed a date for the inquest. No news either of the court case. I don't want to think about it.

What advice can I give myself other than to lean on such imperative clichés as my mother's long ago, 'Always count your blessings, son', or Wilfred's green-days 'nil desperandum' or the stoical motto that I once adopted in days more carefree: 'be visited, expect nothing, and endure'?

Then

It'll be Wilfred's birthday tomorrow. When I was young it was Wilfred, born psychiatrist, to whom I would turn for advice. In some ways he took over my father's paternal duties, becoming responsible, for example, for my education. It was he who decided that I should study Medicine like so many others in the family. Like himself. Like a number of my uncles and cousins. I, a schoolboy at St Illtyd's College, Cardiff, did not demur. I had heard so many gripping stories about medical student life. Indeed I fancied myself walking down Cardiff's Queen Street with a stethoscope sticking out of my pocket! Wilfred reckoned, though, that I should try to study at the newly built Westminster Hospital in London. 'It's the best hospital now in Europe,' he said.

Wilfred also guided me in other ways. It was he, not my father, who took me aside when he saw I had become involved with a particular girlfriend. He gave me advice about sex. 'There's only three things to keep in mind,' my eldest brother maintained. 'One, contraception; two, the unlikely possibility of VD; and three, the emotional entanglements with a girl which follow pleasurable consummations.'

Later, after four-plus years of studying Medicine at Westminster Hospital, feeling the trauma of empathising too much with stricken patients I played truant most of the time, failed my Pathology exam and confessed to Wilfred that I was no longer sure I wanted to practise as a doctor. 'I've had a book of poems published, a play produced, and I'm writing a novel. I think I could make my way as a writer.'

Wilf forcefully insisted that it would be better for me, psychologically, to complete my medical studies. 'If you don't it will mark you for the rest of your life. I speak now not merely as a brother but as a psychiatrist. You'd come to regret it. You'd feel the sting of failure. Listen, in eighteen months or so, if you seriously knuckled down, stopped cutting ward rounds and lectures, read your Conybeare rather than Baudelaire, ceased mucking about in promiscuous Swiss Cottage, you could qualify. *Then* you could make up your mind whether or not to practise Medicine. Think about it. You may be able to go down both roads like Chekhov. Anyhow, Medicine could become the patron of your poetry.' He hesitated. 'By the way, you mentioned you owed your landlady, Mrs Austin, money. I can help you out.'

I did not take Wilfred's advice immediately. For months more I loitered in the cafés of Swiss Cottage and in the pubs of Soho. I rarely ventured into the precincts of Westminster Hospital Medical School. Then I received a threatening note that summoned me to the office of the Dean, the rugby-built surgeon, Mr George MacNab.

The previous year I had joined his firm and had assisted him at an operation. Afterwards he had sighed, 'Well, Abse, some people are good at some things, other people at others!' And, at a ward round, while Mr MacNab had droned on about the case history of the patient we were about to examine I must have fallen into a reverie. Suddenly I realised the rest of the firm were staring at me. Evidently I had been asked a question. They waited. Mr MacNab waited. 'Your name is Abse,' Mr MacNab said sarcastically. 'This is Westminster Hospital. It's Wednesday afternoon. Christmas is coming . . . Now, let me repeat, if a patient's empyema has been drained but the sinus continues to discharge, what would you suggest would be the reason for it?'

MacNab might well remember such incidents when he interviewed me. Would I be expelled for being absent so long from the sick wards of Westminster Hospital? I wouldn't like that. What would my father say? How would Wilfred respond? What would my future be? A freelance writer, having to write things of little interest to me? I could already feel the marks of failure.

I was not the only student sternly brought before the Dean. Mahon who had failed his medical final several times had been called into his office earlier that morning. So had Harrison. Both reassured me, somewhat vainly. MacNab had told Mahon to stop playing football and to study more. And Harrison had been urged to leave his medical books, to play football and get some fresh air!

The Dean did not discuss football with me. He said gently, 'Perhaps you'd like to write poetry and live in a garret, Abse, rather than continue your studies here?' MacNab had intense blue eyes that did not readily blink. I responded, 'I'm not at all keen on garrets, sir.' At last he made a decision and put me under the close supervision of Dr Wynn Williams. Meekly I began to wear the white coat again.

March 17th
Susanna visited me this afternoon and I showed her the poem Nancy Blishen had sent me this morning. She had written it after her husband, Edward, had died and it concerned the birds that had haunted her garden. Immediately my daughter recalled how one open-air day last June soon after Joan's funeral, the dainty robin that had always ventured a hardly measured distance from Joan while she was gardening, had hopped through the open kitchen door into the house and had flown through the hall, up the stairs, into our bedroom.

March 18th

Still falls the cold. And the weathermen forecast that things will not improve next week. Simply, the eastern winds from Siberia will veer north to join those from the Arctic. The trick, I suppose, regarding my own ageing northern weather, is to see the white horse in the snowstorm. Meanwhile spring, famished, slumbers somewhere else and the moon tonight is like a staring owl.

March 21st

I received the proofs of a biography of the poet-priest, R. S. Thomas, in the post this morning. It's by Byron Rogers and the little I've read so far confirms my long-held sense of the man. Though born in Cardiff he had contempt for the 'mongrel' people of South Wales who no longer understood the old language and had relinquished so much of their Welsh heritage.

In 1983 Secker and Warburg gave a party at our house in Ogmore-by-Sea to celebrate the publication of the topographical anthology, *Wales in Verse*. Most of the contributors such as Glyn Jones, John Ormond, John Tripp, Tony Curtis, Gillian Clarke, Robert Minhinnick, Nigel Jenkins, Sally R. Jones, Roland Mathias, Herbert Williams, etc. accepted the invitation. Not R. S. He disdainfully refused to come south to a seaside village which had the cursed sound of Englishness about it. Secker should have invited him to Ogwr — the Welsh name for Ogmore-by-Sea.

John Ormond who had made a BBC film about R. S. Thomas once suggested to me that because of my

Jewish background and because of R. S. Thomas's Church of Wales brand of Christianity, we, though Welsh, were both outsiders in Wales. Perhaps. Outside is a lonely place and R. S. made every attempt to become an insider, to belong, by becoming a vehement Welsh nationalist, by learning the Welsh language, by steeping himself in Welsh legend and Welsh history and by focusing on rustic Wales and its hill farmers for his earlier subject matter.

R. S. Thomas's early poems are unignorable; but it is a late poem of his that comes to my mind now, one where he speaks of the death of his first wife.

A Marriage

We met
            under a shower
of bird-notes.
            Fifty years passed,
Love's moment
            in a world in
servitude to time.
            She was young;
I kissed with my eyes
            closed and opened
them on her wrinkles.
            'Come' said death,
choosing her as his
            partner for
the last dance. And she,
            who in life

> had done everything
> > with a bird's grace,
> opened her bill now
> > for the shedding
> of one sigh no
> > heavier than a feather.

Then

My brother Leo has always surprised me with his unpredictable prejudices. I once asked him what he thought of Robert Maxwell when both he and Maxwell were Labour MPs. 'I don't like him,' Leo had said.

'Why not?'

'He rushes to open a door for you,' Leo remarked pensively. 'I don't care for those who do such things!' On another occasion I heard Leo giving short-shrift judgement of a person simply because the man's mouth turned down at the edges!

I thought of Leo's spot-prejudices when Joan and I encountered R. S. Thomas and his bubbly second wife, Betty, in the hotel in Barcelona. R. S. waited to keep the exit door open for me and I observed that his old handsome countenance had a misanthropic aspect because his mouth turned down at the edges!

Later R. S. Thomas, Gwyneth Lewis and I joined Gareth Alban Davies, the Welsh language poet and Spanish scholar, on the platform of the British Council's Barcelona premises. After the readings to the Catalan audience there was a discussion where R. S. masochistically whined about the great tragedy of his life – that he could not write Welsh poetry, that he did not know the Welsh language well enough to do so, that he felt he betrayed Wales by writing in English, that he was entrapped by his colonial English upbringing. Certainly, in manner and in accent, and in his reserved behaviour, he appeared to be a very English Welshman with a simulated hate of England. But still he was a fine poet.

March 24th

The weather milder, at last. Went to the wardrobe to look for a lighter jacket, actually one particular one that, though quite old, I cared for most. I couldn't find it. Then I remembered – that summer night in June. They cut it to pieces. 'Leave me alone,' I had shouted, but the paramedics (or was it the fireman?) cut it to pieces while I stood bleeding beside the upturned car on the dark M4. They cut it to pieces. 'I'm all right, leave me alone.' They cut it to pieces – the old coat I cared for most.

March 25th

A spring morning in London so David offered to come to Cardiff with me for the day to watch the Bluebirds play Queens Park Rangers. Larne took the same 10.45 train on her way to holiday in Ogmore for a week but I couldn't face even an overnight stay. As the train approached Wales the sky became old and surly with presentiments of rain. In Cardiff itself 'witches and walking sticks' (as the Welsh say) descended from the lowered clouds. I discovered my mackintosh was not rain proof.

Once inside the Stand, damp, sitting in my season-ticket seat – Block D, row M7 – next to friendly familiar City addicts I forgot the incessant rain, pleased to be there after so many months. The usual pigeons had taken shelter but instead white seagulls circled over the green pitch. Then came the reassuring banality of the pre-game ritual – the vigorous tannoy playing 'Men of Harlech' before a manic voice screamed 'SUPPORT THE BOYS, MAKE SOME NOISE'.

I have been to many boring matches. This o–o draw was one of them. Peter Gutmann who occupies a seat in the row behind me, alone among 14,000 fans, found the game of some interest. Even Steve, normally religiously kind said, 'Flippin' 'eck, this is like watching paint drying on a wall.' Both sides, lethargic, played the off-side game. Only the linesman seemed animated, 'Offside? Never. NEVER. Bloody idiot.'

On the return journey I intended to read the book pages of David's Saturday *Guardian*. I knew it carried a poem of mine from *Running Late*. I had written this particular poem, 'The Malham Bird' in 2004 and dedicated it to Joan. The newspaper had been soaked through with rain not tears. I looked across the table at the seat next to David where Joan was not.

The Malham Bird

(For Joan)

That long summer a clarity of marvels
yet no morning News announced the great world
had been reinvented and we were new,
in love — you a Gentile and I a Jew!

Dear wife, remember our first illicit
holiday, the rented room, the hidden beach
in Wales, the tame seagull that seemed a portent,
a love message, as if Dafydd's ghost had sent it?

After our swim we lay on our shadows naked,
more than together, and saw high in the blue
two chalk lines kiss and slowly disappear.
Then the friendly gull swooped down, magnified,
   near.

Now, three grandchildren later, I think of
a black feathered bird, the malham of Eden,
how it took advice, closed its eyes resolute,
when others singing pecked forbidden fruit;

and how, of all the birds, it was not banished
but stayed, lonely, immortal, forever winging
over the vanished gardens of Paradise.

March 27th
During the last few weeks several visitors, Cary Archard,
William and Patricia Oxley, Q, Norman Kreitman, Siân

Williams, have with tactful perspicuity commented on my visible loss of weight. So have my two daughters. In a subtle way they are really saying you look wan and older. I know. I shave and bathe every morning. Radical changes in a person's life can hasten the kinetic ageing process, not least the diminishing vigour of the musculature. Perhaps I'm becoming one of those old crabbed men (R. S. Thomas?) James Reeves somewhat patronisingly wrote about. I insist though that I do not have an offensive smell, Mr Reeves, nor a falsetto voice, though first thing in the morning I do feel soused with age.

Old Crabbed Men

This old crabbed man with his wrinkled, fusty
    clothes
And his offensive smell – who would suppose
That in his day he invented a new rose
Delightful still to a fastidious eye and nose?

That old crabbed man, pattering and absurd,
With a falsetto voice – which of you has heard
How in his youth he mastered the lyric word
And wrote songs as faultless as those of a spring
    bird?

This old crabbed man, sloven of speech and dress,
Was once known among women – who would now
    guess?—
As a lover of the most perfect address,
Reducing the stubbornest beauty to nakedness.

That old crabbed man, a Herod of the first water,
His manhood consumed in bragging, drink and
    slaughter,
The terror of fag, bearer, batman, caddy, porter,
Is the adored of his one infant great-granddaughter.

From such crabbed men – should we not realise?—
Despite their present insupportable guise,
May have been distilled something apt, sweet or wise,
Something pleasing perhaps to former minds or eyes.

Nowadays, where more and more pensioners thrive, it's odd that there should be such a tinkling cult of youth. The present interest in cosmetic plastic surgery tells a wish-fulfilment story, as does the more serious research on foetal stem cells where the hope is not only the replacement of failing tissues and organs but eternal life itself.

Since the first man turned grey the human race has longed for a rejuvenating agent capable of revitalising our lethargic cells. There is a legendary belief that the proximity of young women could revitalise aged men. The Old Testament tells us, in the tale of King David and Abishag (shag?), 'Now King David was old and stricken in years; and they covered him with clothes, but he gat no heat. Wherefore his servants said unto him, Let there be sought for my lord the King a young virgin. So they sought for a fair damsel all through the coasts of Israel, and found Abishag a Shunammite, and brought her to the King. And the damsel was very fair, and cherished the King, and ministered to him: but the

King knew her not.' No wonder, one might add. They shouldn't have chosen a virgin.

I like too the anecdote of Rabelais who wrote of the fountain of youth magician who assured Pantagruel that he made a practice of melting down and refurbishing old ladies – with such magical success that all the pretty girls present had, in fact, been reconditioned in this way, and made in all reports as good as new: looks, figure, elegance, stature, limbs – exactly as they had been at the age of fifteen or sixteen. The only difference was a curious effect on their feet, which remained much shorter than in their first youth – and as a result of this, they much more readily fall on their backs if one gives them a push ... Pantagruel asked the wizard if he couldn't rejuvenate men in the same way. The answer was no. All they need to do is to cohabit with a lady who has been reconditioned ...

The notion that a man may osmotically absorb virtue and youth from a woman is known as gerocomy. In rats gerocomy has been found to work. When a single young female rat was placed amidst ageing males it groomed them, and their physical condition improved so that they survived longer.

I suspect that gerocomy may work in human beings also. It did so for me. Though I don't consider myself to be virtuous I would have been less so if it had not been for the sympathetic unspoken judgements of Joan. And if I look older now surely it's because Joan is no longer here to act as my own magical elixir! Still I find myself wondering, frequently wondering, whether Joan,

truth's gracious secretary, would have approved or disapproved of things I've said recently, or done, or wrote.
Perhaps I was always seeking her esteem.

March 28th
Windy day. I look out of the window and wish I could
paint: the kinetic light on the lawn, the flung birds.
Everything in the garden is alive, moving. Sometimes
it's easy to believe in the disguises of the dead. I wish
I could paint. Surely those who decide to paint land-
scapes begin a new life?

The bullying March winds of yesterday that are now
somewhat calmed have lifted slates from the roof. I
can't remember the name of the builders whom Joan
used to employ. So many blanks in the memory. Is it
increasing age that makes me ask myself more frequently,
where did I put those keys? Did I turn off the gas
oven? Why the hell did I leave my study to walk into
this room? The sludge of incomprehension. I think of
Rob Martinez who when asked on his 102nd birthday,
'What is the secret of a prolonged life?' hesitated, before
finally confessing, 'I used to know the answer to that!'

Many paragraphs in the story of a man's life are so
heavily deleted they cannot even be read by their author.
They are like small flames struck by matches. Blown
out, where have they gone?

March 29th
Joan would have wanted me to go to Robert Woof's
memorial gathering at the National Portrait Gallery.

She would have reminded me how warmly Pamela and Robert Woof had welcomed us when, in June 2004, we had visited Grasmere to give a reading for the Wordsworth Trust.

Robert Woof, who died last autumn of lung cancer, was an eminent scholar who advocated the work of contemporary writing. For instance, he established a poetry programme at Grasmere, including residences for young poets, such as Owen Sheers. Unsurprisingly I met a number of poets last evening at the National Portrait Gallery, among them Seamus Heaney, Anne Stevenson, J. P. Ward, Fleur Adcock and Tony Harrison.

I was amazed that Pamela Woof spoke. (Something that I could not trust myself to do at Joan's memorial.) She held forth for half an hour praising her husband as an outstanding scholar, who experienced the joy of imagination and who caught life on the wing. And there were small moments when I didn't listen to her but thought of Joan and how all my memories, perhaps too much so, began with 'We'.

Before the speeches I was asked by Peter Lucas, Anne Stevenson's husband, how I was coping without Joan. I told him truthfully, 'OK, though I cry three times a day.' It sounded like a prescription – t.d.s.

Then

I had planned to read solo and only poems but because Joan accompanied me to Grasmere I asked her if she would read a short piece of prose. I chose an article about a reading I had given decades earlier, one which had originally been published in *The Poetry Review*. I had the misfortune to be inflicted with a vexatious over-bearing chairman who happened to be a Tory coun-cillor of local celebrity. He was not merely inept but antagonistic towards me and my brother. 'We've heard of Leo Abse's activities. If he came here and put up for election he'd come *last*. After the Communist.' In the *Poetry Review* article that Joan was about to read I had unkindly portrayed the Tory councillor as the pompous fool he was.

Now, just before the 2004 Grasmere reading, I was accosted by a man sitting in the front row. I learnt he was also a Tory councillor! It was too late to direct Joan to another piece of my prose. Robert Woof was already addressing the audience, introducing me.

Given her modest retiring nature Joan never ceased to surprise me when she graced a public platform whether lecturing on art or reading poems. And she had acted out my piece from *The Poetry Review* with a particular cheerful gusto. Her vivacious reading provoked much laughter. I furtively glanced at the Tory councillor in the front row. His ritual smile, I thought, had a certain forced resemblance to the grimace of rigor mortis.

March 30th
The week before last Cary Archard sent me Joan Didion's *The Year of Magical Thinking*, in which he enclosed a note: 'Hope this book will be helpful.' At an earlier date I had read a considered notice of this American author's work in the *London Review of Books* so I knew it was about

bereavement, the mental illness of bereavement. The book still rests on my desk, its pages unopened.

Shall I read it? If it's a self-pitying *cri de cœur* like this manuscript will it ruminate even more tormenting memories? Presumably her experience of perdurable grief will partly resemble my own. The various symptoms of bereavement-illness must be finite in number. Does Joan Didion wake up in the morning, every morning, in oneiric suspense and heartbreak when she realises her partner's not there? The malice of ordinary things such as that unused toothbrush in the bathroom. Tears before breakfast in an empty house perhaps? And later that morning will a sympathetic word from friend or stranger overwhelm her wits to make her swallow hard in the sequel of a little silence? Will she, though now less than usually capable, have to deal with such mundane matters as having to speak to a bank manager and produce the ignominy of a death certificate? Will she in the afternoon receive a phone call from some old acquaintances living abroad who, in ignorance, ask after her partner? At night, after eating alone in insatiate melancholy does she imagine a footstep on the stair?

How often, years gone by has Joan Didion had to write a letter to a new widow about bereavement but not really knowing about it. Sorry. So sorry. So very sorry — and then resumed her life? Icarus drowning not waving as the stately ship sailed on. How often has she, have I, witnessed sudden widows and widowers on a TV news item — this local man thin-lipped; that big-boned man of angry countenance whose wife was found murdered in the nearby woods; this woman weeping whose husband was kidnapped and butchered in Iraq. Sorry. So sorry. So very sorry. And you and I have turned away to drink a cup of tea or coffee. All those millions who have lost their partners, who experience the void of a permanent absence and who, not being frail authors one mile the other side of the moon, do not have this compulsion to write about it.

March 31st

Norman Kreitman, here in London on a brief visit from Edinburgh, called on me this morning. I've known him for ever. We were both medical students at Westminster Hospital in the post-war years. He, now a retired psychiatrist, of course asked me how I was managing. When I confessed that I was keeping a regular appointment with this journal as a therapeutic aid he told me that that is what is recommended sometimes in Japan by psychiatrists. 'Bereaved patients are encouraged to write, to be autobiographical, and to keep a daily diary.' Norman lit his pipe then asked, 'Will you publish it?' I thought how I rewrite some of these pages. That I do so suggests I would. Why else? – though it's true that I do experience ludic pleasure in rewriting, in the choice and in the reshuffling of words. But to publish would be an exposure.

I have not seen Norman since he and his wife, Susan, travelled down from Edinburgh for Joan's memorial. I think he visited me now partly to ensure I hadn't curled up into a somnolent clinical depression. It may be a small restrictive world I live in, its boundaries never far from this house, but it's not all a walk in the cemetery. I may be living copy-cat days but I enjoy my regular rambles into Golders Hill Park and Kenwood, watching football on TV, my weekly chess game with Peter Gutmann, impious conversation with friends, literary gossip, a good film and all the other unshakeable common pleasures, such as food, wine and music. And now spring has, at last, arrived, I can merely open a window to know the intoxication of fresh air. So Norman, I'm not clinically depressed. Merely unhappy.

Then

We were three medical students in an unreliable pulsating car approaching the outskirts of Arles – Norman Kreitman, Clem Cox, and myself. I had not been abroad before. The war had been over three years, yet in Britain we were still on meagre rations and knew only the pleasure of dried eggs! Here agricultural produce seemed abundant, the restaurants inviting. Even the ice cream was real, not cardboard synthetic. The problem was too few francs, and I had no cigarettes left. Norman who had just begun to learn chess brought a set with him. It was boring to play a beginner. We made a deal. He would give me one cigarette every time I played a game with him. Clem observed these frequent brief chess encounters with patient abstract dignity.

We intended to pitch our tent on the shore of the Mediterranean, maybe near St Marie de la Mer where Vincent Van Gogh had described the sea as having the colouring of mackerel altering according to the angles of sunlight. 'You don't always know if it's green or violet,' he wrote to his brother, Theo, 'because the next moment the changing reflections have taken on a tinge of rose or grey.' Norman and I wanted to linger in Arles because we wanted to visit The Yellow House where Van Gogh had once lived and which he had painted. We discovered that it had been bombed out of existence during the war.

My brother Leo and I had recently attended an exhibition of Van Gogh's paintings at the Tate, and Leo believed that the paintings revealed the painter's sexual frustration. 'Probably Van Gogh was impotent,' Leo had said. His letters to Theo which I had read certainly didn't contradict Leo's facile spot diagnosis. I thought often of Van Gogh while Clem, Norman and I, in sprightly jocularity, travelled through the cicada-burring landscape of Provence.

'I have a theory,' I told Norman, solemnly, one evening outside our tent.

'Your move,' Norman said.

'I think Van Gogh was impotent,' I said.

'Your move,' Norman said louder.

'I think his canvases suggest he was impotent,' I continued. 'The cut flowers in the jam jar without water, the bedraggled candles, the sagging chair, the dead fish, the boat stranded on the sand, the sunflower yearning for the sun, the angry wind in the corn never possessing the corn.'

'That's your theory?' asked Norman, obviously unimpressed.

'To tell the truth, it's Leo's,' I admitted.

'Your move,' said Norman.

'Do you know one of Vincent Van Gogh's favourite sayings was that to achieve fame is like ramming the lit end of your cigar into your mouth?'

'Do you want a cigarette or not?'

Finally we pitched our tent not at St Marie de la Mer but on the nearby sands of Le Gran-du-Roi. One night Vincent Van Gogh wrote to Theo, 'I went for a walk by the sea along the empty shore. It was neither gay nor sad. It was ... beautiful. In the blue depth of the sky the stars sparkled greenish, yellow, white, rose, brighter, flashing more like jewels than they do at home – even at Paris – opals, you could call them, emeralds, lapis, rubies, sapphires.'

After that holiday, after our return to London, I met Joan.

April 3rd

My granddaughter Larne, while staying at Ogmore, was contacted by a *Glamorgan Gazette* reporter who wanted to know why the Abse family or their representative hadn't been present at the court. 'What court?' asked Larne.

Nobody had been informed that the court case was scheduled for last Thursday, not even our lawyer, Jill Lansing. Susanna is furious; Keren and David taken aback, somewhat numb. 'It's unheard of,' Jill Lansing exclaimed. She will demand an apology from the Police Authority.

What does it matter? Joan is dead. It seems the woman who drove the Mini Cooper like a bomb into our car pleaded guilty and has been convicted of driving without due care and attention. She had been banned from driving for one year. One year?

April 5th

Blue cloudless sky, liquescent sunlight and spring-like blessings of air drew me, soon after breakfast, into Golders Hill Park. No one was about. I listened to the caw-caw cries of unseen rooks and the incessant grumble of the distant Finchley Road traffic. For long minutes I owned the whole park until a jogger in black singlet and shorts gasped past me. The sun, still low in the blue sky dripped through the nearby trees casting long shadows. As I ascended the gentle sloping path to reach its salient, the empty tennis courts gradually slipped behind and below me. Then, as I continued to move forward, a Wordsworthian parade of daffodils advanced. I sat on a wooden bench and observed their soundless celebration. Soon I was visited by the benign tyranny of a most loved ghost. Was it only one year since Joan and I sat on this same bench? The orchard trees then, were not merely budding, as now in this late spring, but were full of themselves in luxurious blossom. Joan and I shared the world.

To temporarily exorcise her ghost I opened the *Guardian* which I had brought with me and in a desultory way, read about the murder of a Sinn Fein spy in Ireland; of youth unemployment in France leading to riots; of Berlusconi in Italy comparing himself first to Napoleon, then to Jesus; of Hamas's Foreign Minister's declaration:

'There's no room for the state of Israel in this land'; of Iraq, in a political vacuum; of al-Qaeda suspects rotting in Guantanamo. I put the newspaper aside, listened to the caw-caws of the rooks again, the small grumble of distant traffic, and remembered one of the many Wordworth poems that had appealed to Joan.

Lines Written in Early Spring

I heard a thousand blended notes,
While in a grove I sat reclined,
In that secret mood when pleasant thoughts
Bring sad thoughts to the mind,

To her fair works did Nature link
The human soul that through me ran:
And much it grieved my heart to think
What man has made of man.

Through primrose tufts, in that green bower
The periwinkle trailed its wreaths;
And 'tis my faith that every flower
Enjoys the air it breathes.

The birds around me hopped and played.
Their thoughts I cannot measure –
But the least motion which they made,
It seemed a thrill of pleasure.

The budding twigs spread out their fan,
To catch the breezy air;
And I must think, do all I can,
That there was pleasure there.

If this belief from heaven be sent.
If such be Nature's holy plan,
Have I not reason to lament
What man has made of man?

April 6th

During the latter decades as we grew older together Joan usually accompanied me when I gave a poetry reading. Without her solicitous encouragement it felt odd to go forth on my own to the British Library for the launch of *Running Late*. When I ascended from the Tube at Euston I was running early so I went into one of the main station's snack bars to order a croissant. That, I thought, would keep me nutritiously going until a late supper.

Behind a counter two young women, both evidently Asian, served a queue including a tipsy fellifluous Irishman. When it came to his turn to be served however, he swayed into intended politeness to ask, 'Could either of you two foreigners now, somehow manage in a daycent time to make me a real *English* cup of tay? Couldcher?'

After Owen Sheers's likeable reading I, on automatic pilot, turned the pages of *Running Late* avoiding the love poems that concluded the book to read others that for me were less emotionally charged. The benignity of a large applauding poetry-enamoured audience was clearly evident. Well, it did include family and friends! The readings over, Owen Sheers and I sat behind a table to sign our books.

I believe almost 200 people attended the reading so

Siân Williams, who with warmth and care organised the event, along with Hutchinson and Seren the publishers, must have been well pleased.

After a late pizza Susanna drove me back to Hodford Road. It was the end of an occasion I found less stressful than I expected. I said goodbye to Susanna, turned the key in the front door to progress into the odour of nothing, into the waiting empty hall.

April 10th
Mick Felton has sent me a cutting from the *Glamorgan Gazette* with its headline: DEATH: DRIVER AVOIDS PRISON. From the report I learn that the woman who was running up and down the hard shoulder of the M4 hysterically crying: 'I've killed her, I've killed her, I'm sorry, I'm sorry' was only twenty-six years old.

I keep thinking if only we had left that Porthcawl restaurant where we dined with Robert Minhinnick and his wife a few minutes later. If only I had taken a different route back to Ogmore. If only. What a cruel joke the god of luck played so that a Mini Cooper travelling at perhaps 70 mph blindly smashed into our car at such and such a place at such and such a time. Yet the god of luck, in all his perplexing compendium of moods, has been generous to me over many decades. Above all, in this world, in this most strange of meeting places, he steered Joan in the post-war years to where I was waiting for her without knowing who she was. She looked to the right, luckily. I looked to the left, luckily.

Phew!

Do you know that Sumerian proverb
'A man's wife is his destiny'?
But supposing you'd been here,
this most strange of meeting places,
5000 years too early? Or me,
a fraction of a century too late?
No angel with SF wings
would have beckoned,
'This way, madam, this way, sir.'

Have you ever, at a beach,
aimed one small pebble
at another, thrown high, higher?

And though what ends
happily
is never the end,
and though the secret is
there's another secret always,

because this, because that,
because on high the Blessed
were playing ring-a-ring-o'-roses,
because millions of miles below,
during the Rasoumovsky,
the cellist, pizzicati,
played a comic, wrong note,
you looked to the right, luckily,
I looked to the left, luckily.

Then

During the post-war years Poetry-Drama became fashionable. I had succumbed to write such a play myself based on a short story by Balzac. I was too young to realise that it should have remained in the secrecy of a dark drawer. Despite its immaturity, its passages of humourless ornamental language, it was produced by the 28 Group at the Rudolf Steiner Hall in St John's Wood where, not long before, startlingly, Bernice Rubens had played the lead in Oscar Wilde's *Salome*.

After the first night performance of my play I'd arranged a rendezvous with the leading actress Betty D. (At that time my sexual liaisons were cheerfully, though chaotically plural and complicated.) Disgracefully I did not keep that date with Betty for in the audience I spied the graceful twenty-one-year-old Joan Mercer. I was surprised because I believed she, having recently finished her studies at the LSE had arranged to spend a year in France. Hardly a month had passed since we had spent a goodbye night at her lodgings in Belsize Park. It seemed possible then that she would be a fragrance that would inevitably vanish. I was reconciled to never seeing again that look of serious determination briefly visiting her pretty face when she had a passionate opinion to express. But there she was, with her long brown hair tumbling down her straight back, a brown fringe covering her high forehead and her ginger eyes steadily focused on the stage.

In those post-war years an audience would, on occasions, shout out 'author, author' on first nights. I must have had many Swiss Cottage acquaintances there, including two or three medical student friends, for that's what happened. On stage, half-blinded by light, facing the anonymous applause I felt awkward but hoped Joan Mercer would be impressed. She was.

April 11th

Gillian Clarke has invited me to read at the Cardiff International Poetry Prize-giving event on May 11th. I thought initially I would accept, book into an hotel overnight since I couldn't face Ogmore. Over the decades I must have stayed in hundreds of hotels abroad and in Britain, frequently on my own after a poetry reading in this or that city. No big deal, yet now the idea of the insulation of a hotel bedroom without Joan even in my home town makes me feel it would be a joyless venture.

Is that merely an excuse to say, 'No, thank you'? Or is the real reason because I would feel insecure like a pre-puberty boy who has strayed too far from base without a responsible adult in attendance? No, no – that's not the reason. Why should I test myself?

I keep changing my mind. I could stay at the Angel Hotel. It would be comfortable there. Come back to London the next morning. But I think, now, of that occasion when I, a young doctor, had to attend a patient at the Angel. What's that got to do with it? Besides I could stay in the Park Hotel or the Holiday Inn or the Royal. Why not?

I'm displeased with myself. You're not entirely well, Dr Abse. Is all this procrastination a symptom of a bereavement illness or that of post-traumatic stress? Or both? Excuses, excuses. I telephone my regrets. Maybe next year? *Mañana.*

Then

It was my first locum, that summer of 1950, not too long after I qualified. My uncle Max, who practised medicine in Cardiff's Cowbridge Road a few houses away from where Ivor Novello once lived, showed me over his surgery before departing for a three-week holiday in Cyprus. He opened a door of a tall vertical cupboard. 'This is my dispensary,' he said, pointing to huge flasks of different coloured fluids. My uncle had been trained as a chemist before becoming a doctor and took pride in prescribing his patients suitable bottles of medicine. But dispensing medicine had not been part of the Westminster Hospital Medical School syllabus.

'Don't worry,' Uncle said, 'each flask is labelled: *For Nervous Complaints, For Stomachs, For Coughs*, etc., with the appropriate dosage. You'll find the bromide flasks very useful. For the newer drugs you'll have to write out a prescription.'

One of my first patients was staying at the Angel Hotel. From Uncle's clinical notes I gathered he was simply convalescing, taking it easy, recovering from a right spontaneous pneumothorax (a collapsed lung) but he had phoned to ask my uncle to call on him. He was not pleased to see me. In fact he was agitated. And after I had examined him he said coolly, 'When you leave this room, doctor, I'm going to jump out of that window.' The window was open. Down, way below, was the summer Westgate Street.

I spent an hour in the Angel Hotel with that patient. He suffered less from his spontaneous pneumothorax than from a secret bereavement. It was not his wife who had died but a woman who lived in Cardiff and with whom he had had a long on-going affair. Finally I promised to see him again. I did so and brought with me a bottle of my Uncle Max's old-fashioned bromide mixture.

When I think of him now I suppose he *might* have committed suicide. But perhaps suffering a collapsed right lung served as a substitute for it? Over the years my experiences as a doctor have confirmed to me that a collapsed lung, just like a perforating ulcer, can sometimes have a psychogenic origin – such as the stress involved through a radical change in the intrinsic emotional DNA of a man's life.

April 13th

A green hedge. A tall green hedge. The tallest green hedge surely in the world. We were walking beside it, then Joan was climbing a ladder to reach the top. I looked up. The ladder had been elevated much higher than the hedge and Joan precariously balanced herself on it. 'The hedge goes on and on,' she called. The ladder tilted. 'Come down,' I yelled. 'Come down,

Joan.' She could fall. I was alarmed. 'Look,' she replied, 'it goes on and on.' She was much too high. The ladder did not appear to be safe. 'JOAN, COME DOWN NOW,' I commanded and half woke up in a strange anxiety. The bedroom was dark. I stretched my arm to the other side of the bed, to that empty area of irrevocable absence. I turned away from it, lay on my side, stared for a moment at the muffled lamp post light behind the curtains, then tried to go to sleep.

April 16th

It's a moody grey Sunday evening and the light is already fading. I have been writing letters but now I think of you, Joan, as I look up from this desk at the different objects decorating this room: the painting above the TV by your father; the different shaped vases, including the one we brought back from Mexico; the plate of pebbles pilfered from Ogmore beach; the photograph of Ogmore taken by Pat Wain – other pieces too which you once decided to place there or there.

The havoc of memories! Is it the faint odour, the insinuations of those blue hyacinths in the vase on the windowsill that made me look up, distracted, and which transported me back? Or less likely, did some stranger in the losing road outside whistle our own street code-call, those few divine plangent bars from the adagio of Schubert's *Quintet* for two cellos? I hear you say, 'Wrong again, Emily' – that Dylan Thomas remark which we appropriated for our small private collection of family sayings.

Lists! I'm thinking lists of remembrance-scenes and should stop, knowing how pure sentiment may sugar itself over and mush into the bacterial. Even so, self-indulgent, I continue. Look, we are in the National Gallery of Wales and you take me by the arm to stand pensively before that Poussin painting; we are returning from the high sand dunes of Ogmore after being passion's slaves – there is a sunset; we are at Cardiff's Roath Park Lake staring at the heavily falling thick white ribbons of the incessant waterfall and I take your living hand. We are together wherever we are and soon we'll go back, probably on such a Sunday evening as this, not yet married, to our small flat in London's Belsize Square and I am twenty-six and you are twenty-three. I shall write a poem called 'Sunday Evening' and you will like it well enough to type it out for me.

Sunday Evening

Loved not for themselves those tenors who sing
arias from *Aida* on horned, tinny
gramophones – but because they take a man back
to a half-forgotten thing.

We, transported by this evening loaded
with a song recorded by Caruso,
recall some other place, another time,
now charmingly outmoded.

What, for wrong motives, too often is approved
proves we once existed, becomes mere flattery
– then it's ourselves whom we are listening to,
and, by hearing, we are moved.

To know, haunted, this echo too will fade
with fresh alliteration of the leaves,
as more rain, indistinct, drags down the sky
like a sense of gloom mislaid.

Dear classic, melodic absences
how stringently debarred, kept out of mind,
till some genius on a gramophone
holes defences, breaks all fences.

What lives in a man and calls him back
and back through desolate Sunday evenings?
Indescribable, oh faint generic name:
sweet taste, bitter lack.

April 17th

My morning walk yesterday took me yet again into
sunlit Golders Hill Park. Leaving the house I choose
different directions but frequently find myself in the
park – rather like when the kids were small, in order
to give Joan space, I would bundle the three of them
into our Morris Minor and promise them a mystery
tour which however always, unintentionally, ended up
at Alexandra Palace.

Yesterday, in the walled garden, I discovered something wonderful had happened overnight. The two

adjacent magnolia trees had dressed up in their white-wedding finery. Such beautiful vulgarity!

There used to be a wooden bench placed exactly beneath those two magnolias, which, so close together, appeared to be enjoying marital bliss! It is some twenty years or so now since I wrote in the local *Ham and High* that whoever rested on that bench overnight while the trees were in ferocious blossom would become immortal. Soon after, the park authorities removed the bench.

April 18th
Good news about *Ash on a Young Man's Sleeve*. The Library of Wales (sponsored by the Welsh Assembly) wish to include it in their new prestigious classic series. So far the five books selected (just published) are all by dead authors. I'm reminded of that wartime comedian Vic Oliver who used to scrape a few discordant notes on his violin and would stop to say mournfully, 'Corelli is dead, Tartini is dead, Paganini is dead . . . I don't feel so great myself.'

Ash on a Young Man's Sleeve, which I began to write while still a medical student, was first published by Hutchinson in 1954. I had written an autobiographical short story which Muriel Spark and Derek Stanford accepted for a literary magazine they were then co-editing. Thus encouraged I decided to extend this fiction to book length. It was a prose holiday taken away from working on poems – though, at one time, I had to put all writing aside when I took my final examinations in Medicine before and during June 1950.

I based the characters in my fictional book on a number of my eccentric family members: 'Uncle Bertie' for instance, the tallest, most well built and pugnacious of my father's three brothers. Bertie, as I called him, in real life was ready to pick a fight at any and every vexatious opportunity. Some fifteen years ago I was asked if a fellow with my surname who managed a cinema during the 1930s in the Welsh valleys was a relative of mine. 'This fellow,' my ageing interlocutor continued, 'would come on to the little stage before the programme began. Every Saturday night, he'd take off his coat, roll up his sleeves and shout, "If anybody wants a fight let's 'ave it now, by 'ere, before the show starts, not afterwards."'

'That must have been my Uncle Bertie,' I confessed. 'Did anyone take him on?'

'Not when I was there. A pity.'

Uncle Bertie has been dead these many years. All my many uncles and aunts are dead. Most of the characters I introduced into *Ash on a Young Man's Sleeve* from the comical cast of real life are dead. And though, Vic Oliver, I don't feel so good myself, I'm mighty pleased the Library of Wales will allow them, along with the purely fictional ones, to live out their antics, their troubles and triumphs, on the page a little longer.

Then

Hutchinson had accepted my second book of poems and in 1952 I mentioned to them I had written three quarters of a prose book which I intended to call *Ash on a Young Man's Sleeve*. Richard Church, Hutchinson's literary adviser, asked to see the unfinished manuscript.

'I'm not sure you should send off that last bit you've written,' said Joan. 'I mean about Uncle Bertie and the cat.'

'It's funny,' I insisted.

When, delighted with myself, I had read out the piece I had written about Bertie shooting the cat dead, Joan instead of laughing as I fully expected her to, cried out, 'Oh no!' Then, sensing my disappointment at her reaction, she continued 'It's OK. I expect most people will find that scene comical but . . .'

BUT. That's a word authors do not wish to hear. When 'but' is uttered you know you have failed. But . . . but . . . the Uncle Bertie/dead cat scene still makes me smile. Comedy, as Coleridge once wrote, is the blossom of the nettle. Or something like that.

Weeks later I received a note from Richard Church inviting me to lunch at the Savile Club. I wore a tie for the occasion and set forth anxiously wondering what would be his response to my unfinished manuscript.

In the dining hall Richard Church did not talk about my book. He chatted to me about literary matters — how he had been Dylan Thomas's editor when he had worked for Dent; about world events, the Kenyan Mau Mau, the first atomic bomb tested by Britain — but he said not one word about *Ash*. Finally he rose from the table and invited me into another smaller room to take coffee.

Now, surely, I thought, he will discuss my manu-script, but as we drank coffee he remarked about how the Government would shortly end rationing; about all the dead in a recent train crash in suburban Harrow; about Anne Frank's diary which had recently been published. At last, Richard Church said, 'About your book . . .' He looked towards the door. 'Ah,' he continued, 'did you see who just came in? Harold Hobson. The drama critic.' He smiled to himself remembering some-thing, some incident I presumed that involved Harold Hobson. Then once more, he came into focus as he repeated, 'I was saying about your book . . . oh, for heaven's sake, look there's Ralph Richardson.' I did not pay sufficient attention to Richard Church's laudatory opinions about Richardson's acting. Some ten minutes went by before he sighed, 'I must go. About your book. One author can't tell another author what to do.' Perhaps that's true. Yet he could have warned me what not to do.

Back in our Belsize Park flat I told Joan how I had had a free lunch and did she know that Jomo Kenyatta, the President of the Kenyan African Union, had been arrested?

April 21st
One of those days, the blankness of it — as if I had tried to open a door and the knob came away in my hand. Nobody called. I've done bugger all except read

the morning newspaper and shop briefly in Sainsbury's.
Now it's already late afternoon and I can hear the silence.

I once wrote, 'Love read this though it has little
meaning/for by reading this you give me meaning.' You,
Joan, of course cannot oblige and I ponder on my own
present circumscribed existence. Others, suffering some
irreplaceable loss manage to glimpse something numinous within their being, something that is 'Not I' as
Martin Buber would put it. He described how when
he was eleven years of age he stroked the neck of a
dapple-grey horse and experienced 'a deeply stirring
happening'. He asserted, 'What I experienced in touch
with the animal was the Other, the immense otherness
of the Other which did not remain strange like the
otherness of the ox and the ram ... When I stroked
the mighty mane, sometimes marvellously smooth-
combed, at other times just as astonishingly wild, and
felt the life beneath my hand, it was as though the
element of vitality itself bordered on my skin, something that was not I, something certainly not akin to
me, palpably the other, not just another, really the Other
itself ...'

Some people unable to discover such religious solace
may savage themselves in an opiate variety of ways,
functioning instinctively, having, like all of us, a narrow
range of volition. I hope I'm not being self-destructive –
my suicide potential is low as I've now found out
– nor am I likely to seek within for an impossible
revelation or, over-active, climb a mountain to blow a
ram's horn. All I can do is utter words, some washed

in tears, though I know they may affect the speaker more than the hearer.

There is a Midrashic saying that when a man enters the world his little hands are clenched as if to challenge the future storms and vicissitudes of life, but when he exits from the world defeated his hands are wide open. I look at my hands. They are neither clenched nor open. But where I am now is at a cul-de-sac. When shall I be less static, will I ever be again, a man alive, a whole man alive?

April 23rd
A birthday lunch with Ania, Reva and Leo, who is now a sparky eighty-nine. As soon as we meet he tells me energetically that his book on Daniel Defoe is to be published next November and that he has now written 10,000 words already on Jubal, the first musician. 'Music,' he asserts with characteristic analytical dogmatism, 'began with a fart.'

Before long, acting the elder bother, he advises me to seize the day. 'That's what you should do. Look neither back nor forward. *Carpe diem.*'

It is not possible to disinherit the past, nor do I want to. Only yesterday searching for a particular book on Thomas Hardy by Robert Gittings I discovered it finally in Joan's study. I opened it up only to see the inscription on the flyleaf: *For Dannie (1951–1976). In cele-bration of twenty-five years of legal happiness. Joan.* Sometimes the past comes at you with a sledgehammer. But, to quote, there are other 'Sometimes'.

Sometimes things don't go, after all,
from bad to worse. Some years, muscadel
faces down frost; green thrives; the crops don't fail.
Sometimes a man aims high, and all goes well.

A people sometimes will step back from war,
elect an honest man, decide they care
enough, that they can't leave some stranger poor.
Some men become what they were born for.

Sometimes our best efforts do not go
amiss; sometimes we do as we meant to.
The sun will sometimes melt a field of sorrow
that seemed hard frozen: may it happen for you.

April 25th
Arriving earlier than I intended for my weekly gym stint
at the Royal Free Hospital's recreation club I joined
two of the group who were sitting at a table in the
cafeteria, Leon, a University lecturer, and Bill, an ex-
London cab driver. The conversation drifted and I learnt
how, at present, conservationists wish to introduce
adders into London's unused quarries and wild suburban
landfill sites. Apparently the greater London population of snakes are not breeding enough and are in danger
of extinction.

'They should leave well alone,' Bill argued. 'Them
adders are really venomous. They'll be seeing more
patients in the casualty department.'

'You don't hear about fatalities from adder bites,'
Leon said.

'They had a big problem in the Highlands, a few years ago,' Bill insisted. 'Campers, I mean. They went for the dogs, see.'

'What?'

'Them adders killed the dogs.'

'Killed the dogs?'

'They were a strongly vicious type of vipers.'

'Adders.'

'Same thing. There were a lotta dead dogs scattered in the Highlands a coupla years ago. Them adders lived in the heather.'

Leon reminded us that while the snake does not get a great press in the Bible, the medical profession has borrowed the emblem of the snake from the healing god, Asklepios.

What is it about the snake that makes man attribute to it transcendental powers for good or evil? We respond to it psychically as more than just a phallic symbol. We recognise, surely, its chthonic message. When I visited Nashville, Tennessee, some years ago, I heard of a local cult where a 'spiritual' group induced a self-mesmerising hysteria by clapping hands, by chanting, and by passing a poisonous snake from hand to hand though this led to fatalities. Ruskin refers to the serpent as 'a divine hieroglyph of the demoniac powers of the earth' and as 'the clothed power of the dust':

There are myriads lower than this, and more loath-some, in the scale of being; the links between dead matter and animation drift everywhere unseen. But it is the strength of the base element that is so dreadful in the serpent; it is the very omnipotence of the earth. That rivulet of smooth silver – how does it flow, think you? It literally rows the earth, with every scale for an oar; it bites the dust with the ridges of its body. Watch it, when it moves slowly: – A wave, but without wind! a current but with no fall! all the body moving at the same instant, yet some of it to one side, some to another, or some forward, and the rest of the coil backwards; but all with the same calm will and equal way – no contraction, no extension; one soundless, causeless march of sequent rings, and spectral procession of spotted dust, with dissolution in its fangs, dislocation in its coils. Startle it; – the winding stream will become a twisted arrow; – the wave of poisoned life will lash through the grass like a cast lance. It scarcely breathes with its one lung (the other shrivelled and abortive); it is passive to the sun and shade, and is cold or hot like a stone; yet, 'it can outclimb the monkey, outswim the fish, outleap the jerboa, outwrestle the athlete, and crush the tiger.' It is a divine hieroglyph of the demoniac power of the earth – of the entire earthly nature. As the bird is the clothed power of the air, so this is the clothed power of the dust; as the bird is the symbol of the spirit of life, so this of the grasp and sting of death.

Then

That August summer of 1972 we had rented a house situated on the arid sloping hills high above the seaside Spanish village of Nerja. Joan and the children had travelled there ahead of me as I was still occupied at

the chest clinic. But now my holiday, too, was about
to begin. I would fly from Heathrow to Malaga and
join them. Beforehand, while breakfasting, I listened
to a beguiling Saturday talk on the radio about the
adders of the Sussex Downs. I learnt how they rarely
cause fatalities, of the intricacies of their sex life and
of the many myths about them. An adder, by startling
a soldier into precipitous lethal action, signalled the
beginning of the Battle of Camlann during which King
Arthur is reputed to have died. During the Middle
Ages the minced flesh of adders, when consumed, was
supposed to act as a rejuvenating cure. Later, adder
skins were wrapped about aching joints to alleviate
rheumatism.

So, armed with such stunning expert knowledge to
Nerja then I came. The holiday house (well appointed
as the *Sunday Times* advert had indicated) was situated
on the declivous terrain of the mountain range high
above the Spanish village and was somewhat isolated.

'I wonder,' I said to Joan, out of earshot of the children, 'if we should be concerned about snakes here?'

'We're plagued with flies,' Joan complained. 'The
Sunday Times didn't tell us about that.'

'Do you know, Joan, an adder started the Battle of
Camlann.'

'What?'

I then began to display, modestly, my profound snake-
scholarship but Joan did not seem impressed. 'There's
little we can do about these flies,' she said.

She, too, became snake-conscious the next morning.

I, still in my pyjamas, had opened the front door and was immediately confronted by the puissant sight of a bloody beheaded snake. It lay there like the detritus of some sacrificial ritual. 'Joan,' I called, 'there's a snake here.' At first she did not respond thinking that I was simply joking with the unbuttoned gaiety of a holiday. 'It's a dead snake,' I shouted. At last she came to the porch to view the severed snake and the scattered blood. 'For heaven's sake!' Then common sense usurped stranger imaginings, and Joan suggested that perhaps a dog had placed the two and a half foot snake on our porch. Certainly not someone wishing us, in the house, ravenous ill will. 'Or a cat,' I added unconvinced, and thought how coincidences happen all the time – what was the word Jung used? Synchronicity. All that talk the previous evening about snakes . . .

But when the next morning, Monday, I unbolted the front door I was disconcerted to see yet another snake freshly decapitated.

'This didn't happen before I came, did it?' I asked Joan.

'Of course not.'

Tuesday morning a third snake on the porch. What? Or who and with what devilry? 'I've not seen a dog. But it must be a dog,' Joan argued. Wednesday morning, relief. No eerie message on the porch. Nor on Thursday morning; but when I unbolted the back door I saw a baby snake beheaded.

The rest of our holiday, no snake, decapitated or otherwise, appeared.

April 28th

A letter from Ann Haile, a senior crown prosecutor in charge of the case against the young woman who drove her car into our Nissan. In it she confirms that the defendant had at first pleaded not guilty. Then 'the defence had instructed their own collusion expert and we were awaiting his report'.

'Collusion expert'? What a classical Freudian slip!

Ann Haile apologises, as the police have already done, for their failure to let me know when the court case was proceeding. 'At the hearing of March 30th 2006,' Ann Haile writes, 'it was anticipated that the matter would be set down for a trial, however, at this hearing the defendant entered a guilty plea before District Judge Williams. The district judge immediately passed sentence upon the defendant, fining her £1200 with £250 costs and disqualifying her from driving for twelve months and stating that her eyesight will be raised with the DVLA before the return of her driving licence . . .'

I don't feel the need to acknowledge this letter of apology. Reading it, I feel I'm somewhere on the way to somewhere else. Not every scene of remembrance – so often, so many – follows from an external stimulus.

April 29th

A BBC producer had attended the reading at the British Library and he subsequently invited me to read three poems for the Radio 3 programme, *The Verb*. 'You may choose the poems,' he said.

So, in a studio at Broadcasting House, Portland Place,

I eschewed selecting any of the love poems I had
addressed to Joan but chose one from *Running Late* instead
called 'Piano', since it was only included in the book
because of Joan's persistence.

Piano

At 66 Sandringham Crescent
an upright piano was being eased down
a long flight of stairs by three men
all wearing off-white overalls.
Backward, staccato, two stepped
descending
   one
      stair
        at
          a
            time
till the taller of the two men
began to collapse in slow

slow   slow motion
and the piano
leapt
   to the hallway's rising floor
crashing its memories of music:
simple tunes such as 3 Blind Mice,
as well as great meaningful sonatas
of profundity and faraway,
into a scattered anarchic jigsaw
of free-loving volatile
meaningless sounds
fading

till the stricken piano
lost its memory entirely.

After the ambulance arrived (too late)
one removal man lit a cigarette
and sensing the wide-awake stare
of the householder

tapped the grey ash, with great delicacy,
into the hollow of his cupped left hand.

Then

Joan had typed out the manuscript of *Running Late*
and said, 'You've left out "Piano".' I thought perhaps
its simple typographical pattern was tiresome, too
easy.

'No, no,' she argued, 'it's appropriate.'

She persuaded me to add the poem to the manuscript because she felt it accurately described a quirk
of human behaviour – the removal man's gesture, his
sense of what is proper though seemingly absurd and
minor in the face of a tragic accident.

'Besides,' Joan continued, 'the word "ash" in that
context has an apt connotation.'

Now I flashback again to the fatal car accident on
the M4 and the bewildering quirks of behaviour of all
those bystanders, not least the young woman running
up and down, running up and down, beside the
motorway shouting out her inadequate 'I'm sorry, I'm
sorry' while the fireman wrestled with me.

May 1st

Last weekend I assessed my neglected bank statements and now wonder whether I should cancel a few of the many direct debits favouring charities and organisations which Joan supported. Not CND though. Joan not only joined their protest marches, but at one period in her life, along with another CND acquaintance, would distribute propaganda pamphlets on Saturday mornings. They would stand there, rain or shine, on the corner of Golders Green and Finchley Road outside the obscene temple of grandiose Lloyds Bank. Sometimes I would pass her by with my eyebrows raised and my occasional remarks about how small political individual gestures would go unheeded. But twenty years ago, after the Chernobyl disaster (much in the news at present), she applauded mightily when I wrote, 'I wonder now, once again, in the name of the God others believe in, how much longer will so-called civilised nations absurdly pile up unusable nuclear weapons and to what hell will Man be consigned if, accidentally or purposefully, radioactive winds sail in from places other than Chernobyl?'

Recent reports published indicate that more than 30,000 people are likely to die of cancers as the result of radiation exposure at Chernobyl twenty years ago. Already half a million have died because of the catastrophe, though the UN's International Atomic Energy Agency and the World Health Organisation dispute these figures. I recall my fears when days after the news of the disaster, I observed the wind was blowing from the east. Joan and I happened to be staying at Ogmore during that time. Soon I wrote in my journal.

This morning (May 4th) an east wind was blowing so vigorously in Ogmore that our wooden gate had been thrust open. From the bedroom window I could see that a ewe with two lambs had trespassed into our garden. They were munching the daffodils and narcissi, a nice, forbidden, wicked breakfast. I rushed downstairs, still in my pyjamas, to shoo them out.

As I closed the gate behind them I thought more of the east wind than the sheep. Probably it was bearing invisible death-seeds from Chernobyl. Perhaps radioactive raindrops were sipped from the daffodil cups by the ewe and the lambs. Information, so far, is meagre. In any case, who can believe the complacent, stealthy, reassuring voices of experts and politicians? How much has been covered up before, how much will be told to us now? Will radioactive iodine be taken up by small, thirsty thyroid glands? What about my new granddaughter and all those like her from Ogmore-by-Sea to the Ukraine and beyond where Prometheus is still chained to his rock while the vulture eats his liver?

Last Friday in Cardiff, I visited Llandaff Cathedral. I just happened to be nearby, so popped in as I used to as a boy, passing the yellow celandines beneath the yew tree. Inside soaring spaces of worship – Jewish, Muslim or Christian – I feel not just secular but utterly estranged like one without history or memory. Once more, numb, I observed Epstein's dominating aluminium resurrected Christ. And it was springtime, springtime in the real world and all seemingly dead things were coming alive again though a cancer sailed in from Chernobyl.

Inside the cathedral, I ambled towards the Lady Chapel reredos where, on either side of the sculpted Madonna, six niches are filled with gold-leafed wreathes of wild flowers. In Welsh, dozens of flowers are named after the Virgin, as is proper in a nation that reveres the Mam of the family. The marigold is called *Gold Mair* – Mary's gold; the buttercup, Mary's sweat; the briar rose, Mary's briar; the foxglove, Mary's thimble; the monkshood, Mary's slipper; the cowslip, Mary's primrose; and the snowdrop, Mary's taper. *Tapr Mair.*

If a man believed in a deity, any deity, goddess, god or God, he would in that cathedral, have prayed in English or Welsh or no language at all, for the neutralisation of the death wind. And in Ogmore, this morning, as I stood in my pyjamas while the opera-dramatic clouds, grey, cream, or frowning darker, tracked so visibly westward, my own lips moved.

Because it is the twentieth anniversary of the catastrophe there is much media discussion about its devastating legacy – about the sinister exclusion zone in the shadow of the monumental tomb that buries the invisible tyrannical god and his death rays. His background radiation has left a town deserted, its houses empty of people, its public buildings, its post office, its cinema. Apparently animals ignorantly run around the streets, including wild horses. How disgusting it is that tourists can go to Chernobyl. A travel agency offers a day-long tour of the depopulated area for 340 dollars.

Chernobyl is a real warning from history that the improbable can and does happen.

May 3rd

It is not long past 6 a.m. and the sun in slow motion is clearing the rooftops opposite. Its light settles placidly on the near hedges, invades the leafy suburban trees. It pins dazzling metallic silvery stars on to the parked cars adjacent to the pavements. It is so quiet. No bird song. No moving traffic. No sound in this house either. Silence listens to silence, and, impossibly, I wish. I wish Joan would come into this room and say (I unintentionally wrote 'stay' not 'say'), 'Stop writing, Dannie. Come and have breakfast.'

I didn't imagine it like this. I had assumed that I would go first. Women generally live longer than men. 'By five years generally so that makes you eight years younger than me,' I used to tease Joan. I had arranged our financial affairs in her favour should she have been left a widow and I ignored her occasional scold, 'I don't know how you'd manage without me. You really should learn, at least, how to cook properly!' To which I always replied, 'Didn't I look after us well when you broke your ankle at Ogmore?' Silence listens to silence. Authors, poets, are supposed to be imaginative people but I didn't, couldn't picture my life without Joan. Everything is so other. The very silence has changed. It is the silence of the abyss. Frequently Joan would be working or reading upstairs in her book-lined study and I would be here in the front room downstairs –

the silence of then was not like this silence of now.

There are so many different qualities and varieties of silence: the breathless silence that follows a war explosion; the stony silence of a religious sanctuary; the almost intolerable silence of a remembrance at certain football matches before a piercing whistle blows and the crowd, the crowd of humans, shout out and applaud in relief. There is the silence I have heard through my stethoscope: the silence between two heartbeats and the commanding silence when there is no heartbeat at all.

There is also the agreeable, comfortable silence of two people together, two people who love each other and who have lived together for years. I knew that silence. I think another unknowable silence inhabits us all, a silence that we own uniquely from the night we were born. When in those rarer instances, when we are utterly thoughtless and at the same time are able to hush the clamour that our own senses make, then we may have hints of it — that different unfathomable silence separated from the empire of silence outside.

It might alter with circumstances and with our advancing years so that some carry it within themselves with difficulty. They begin to talk talk talk. That troublesome silence may mutate into the silence of Dread.

The most silent man I have ever known was Arthur Jacobs, a gifted Scots-Jewish poet who lived for a time near our house in Golders Green. I do believe his quietude was as troublesome to himself as it was occasionally to others. Most would ascribe his plural silences to shyness. Others thought he was wise and couldn't

be bothered to discuss trifles as most of us do. And,
doubtless, others believed he was only like the Prince
of Libya that Cavafy wrote about.

Aristomenis, son of Menelaos,
the Prince from Western Libya,
was generally liked in Alexandria
during the ten days he spent there.
In keeping with his name, his dress was also properly
    Greek.
He received honours gladly,
but he didn't solicit them; he was unassuming
He bought Greek books,
especially history and philosophy.
Above all he spoke very little.
Word spread that he must be a profound thinker,
and men like that naturally don't speak very much.

He wasn't a profound thinker or anything at all —
just a piddling, laughable man.
He assumed a Greek name, dressed like the Greeks,
learned to behave more or less like a Greek;
and all the time he was terrified he'd spoil
his reasonably good image
by coming out with some barbaric howlers in Greek
and the Alexandrians, bastards that they are,
would start in their normal way to make fun of him.

This was why he limited himself to a few words,
terribly careful of his syntax and pronunciation;
and he almost went out of his mind, having
so much talk bottled up inside him.

Then

Joan in the hall answered the knock on the front door. I heard her say, 'Come in, Arthur.' I guessed that it was the solitary Arthur Jacobs again standing in the porch intimidatingly silent. Soon she ushered Arthur into our living room where I happened to be reading. 'Arthur's here to see you,' Joan smiled. 'I'll make you some coffee.'

It was the same routine. I asked, 'How are you, Arthur?' He mumbled OK and sat down opposite me as if he were about to be interviewed. After a further disinfectant silence I asked what I knew he wanted me to ask: 'Have you been writing poems, Arthur?'

'No, er, well.'

A pause. A hush.

'Have you been to Newcastle lately?'

'Yes.'

'Did you see Jon Silkin?'

Here our dialogue varied. Arthur sometimes said yes, sometimes no. If he said 'yes' I would add, 'Did he take a poem or two of yours for *Stand*?' To which, sometimes, blushing, he would nod his yes or his no.

Arthur's inward silence was more than mere shyness. Nor did he truly resemble Cafavy's Prince of Western Libya. He seemed to invite questions but would be reluctant to answer. His poems were a coded holograph of his inward inaudibility, a silence expressed in language, terse, hesitant, measured, and on occasions, wryly, satirically, humorous in a Heine/Brechtian manner.

Travelling Abroad

Documents, scrutinies, barriers,
Everywhere I pass through them,
It seems, without difficulty.
Nothing jars, nothing slips out of place,
Authority is satisfied by my credentials.

Really, it must represent some peak
Of achievement, from a Jewish
Point of view, that is.
          What a time
It's taken to bring me
To this sort of freedom,
What tolls have been paid
To let me come
          to this kind
Of passage.
I can appreciate it,
          believe me,
I can appreciate

But I find myself wondering,
As I sit at this café table
          over
A good glass of beer,
Why I don't feel something more
          like gratitude,
Why there's some form of acceptance
I don't grasp.

In 1994, too early, Arthur died but not before, as
Anthony Rudolf wrote in the *Independent* obituary

column, 'he had close friendships with several men and women who . . . honoured his strangeness, who mitigated his loneliness, who admired his hard-won work . . .' I think of Joan coming into the room with coffee and biscuits, asking, 'How are you, Arthur?' A soft Scot voice answering, 'OK.'

May 4th

Happily the weather has unerringly turned around towards summer. In our back garden, the old apple tree which last year we thought might be on its last crutch, now is untouched by the mundane. It has the look of one enobled, crowned with a prodigious flurry of pink-white blossom. So many flowers that Joan planted have triumphantly made their entrance while the daffodils, faded ballerinas, exit with bowed heads.

On such a day as this it should be a commanding duty to change loneliness into solitude. And I realise that it is absurd that, in sloth, I lounge around and about here, in London, when I could be walking beside the open-air sea at Ogmore. I know though, I am too much a prisoner of the past and would feel even lonelier at Ogmore where the incoming waves relentlessly collapse on the sand and shingle to whisper: She, She, She. I must rouse myself. I shall leave this desk and visit the Church Hall around the corner in Rodborough Road where there is a voting booth for the local elections. No doubt I shall see again droppings of pink May blossom in the gutter like torn

bits of the *Financial Times*, bump into some good neighbours, and after voting, indulge in brief exciting
conversations about the blessings of the weather and
the threatened closure of the busy Golders Green Post
Office.

May 5th

I wake up to one of those flawless beautiful mornings
in England that English poets always rhapsodise about.
After Browning etc., Laurie Lee's lyrical poem, 'Day of
these Days' comes to mind. It is a poem that I've heard
Laurie read, or rather lullaby, scores of times for we
were often on tour together during the 1960s. He would
introduce it with the same patter in that gravelly burring
accent of his. As if confessing a secret, he would drawl,
'I wrote this poem on the top deck of a no. 88 bus
while I was travelling from Trafalgar Square to a mile
south of Westminster. At that time the journey cost
me threepence. If I wrote the same poem today it would
cost me . . . ninepence!' Then he would push his glasses
up the bridge of his nose and announce, 'Day of these
Days'.

> Such a morning it is when love
> leans through geranium windows
> and calls with a cockerel's tongue.
>
> When red-haired girls scamper like roses
> over the rain-green grass,
> and the sun drips honey.

When hedgerows grow venerable,
berries dry black as blood,
and holes suck in their bees.

Such a morning it is when mice
run whispering from the church,
dragging dropped ears of harvest.

When the partridge draws back his spring
and shoots like a buzzing arrow
over grained and mahogany fields.

When no table is bare,
and no breast dry,
and the tramp feeds off ribs of rabbit.

Such a day it is when time
piles up the hill like pumpkins,
and the streams run golden.

When all men smell good,
and the cheeks of girls
are as baked bread to the mouth.

As bread and beanflowers
the touch of their lips,
and their white teeth sweeter than cucumbers.

More often than not Laurie would continue his seductive reading by relating how one day he happened to be standing near the World's End pub in Chelsea when a schoolgirl accosted him. 'Are you Laurie Lee?' the girl asked abruptly.

'Yes.'

'Did you write a poem called "Apples"?'

'Yes.'

'My teacher made me learn it!' the girl accused.

'We spent,' Laurie would add conspiratorially, 'a moment of scowling intimacy together.'

I never tired of hearing Laurie Lee's coloured soap-bubble anecdotes, nor did I become irritated by his schoolboy naughtiness. Once after returning from one of Jeremy Robson's Poetry and Jazz Concerts at Aberystwyth he planted a pair of black knickers (where did he get them from?) in my luggage which, on my return home, could have caused me trouble with Joan. And when we played a word game, which we frequently did on trains to pass time, he would cheat though we only gambled for shillings. 'You cheated,' I'd protest. 'Yes,' he'd agree disarmingly, 'I had to. You were winning!'

May 6th

Last night I dreamt I was parking the car at Ogmore when another car, powerfully leaving the kerb simultaneously, cut across me causing minor damage only — a wing mirror smashed etc. As far as I can recall, it is the first time since the accident last June that I have dreamt of a car crash.

May 7th

Last week I gave readings at different London bookshops to promote the sales of *Running Late*. I turned the pages of the book to the less personal poems and I discovered that I was pleasured by reinhabiting them! I was even mildly pleased to engage in the necessary idle chatter while I signed books, but afterwards, scuddling away, I felt moments of dejection as I took a late supper alone in an Edward Hopper restaurant and afterwards sat at home, skewed, staring at the futile images on the TV screen. There was no Joan to reassure me with, 'You were OK' or 'It was fine but you read some of the poems too quickly.'

Climbing the stairs to go to bed last night I thought of the earlier event at the Palmers Green Bookshop and the affirmative poem with which I had concluded the reading:

Valediction

> In this exile people call old age
> I live between nostalgia and rage.
> This is the land of fools and fear.
> Thanks be. I'm lucky to be here.

May 8th

My Sunday morning walk led me predictably to the azaleas and the first bluebells of Golders Hill Park. I had reached the orchard in blossom but I was still within earshot of the thud and thud of the tennis courts when I saw a small grey-haired, very old lady determinedly coming towards me. The focus of her eyes told me I was about to be addressed.

'Mr Abse?'

'Yes.'

'Excuse me, Mr Abse. I meant to write to you when I heard that your wife had died.'

'Thank you.'

She hesitated. She was going to say something more, something important. 'My husband died last December,' she said.

'I'm sorry. It's not easy, is it?'

'This park is helpful,' she said.

'It is. Do you live near here?'

'Yes. In Dunstan Road.'

I think she wanted to say more but couldn't. Instead the next moment the puny old lady was in my arms. I found myself giving this stranger a brief warm hug. Then she took the path that would overlook the tennis courts and I climbed towards the pretty colours of the azaleas thinking of all the lonely old widows in the world. And of course the old widowers too.

The Origin of Music

When I was a medical student
I stole two femurs of a baby
from the Pathology Specimen Room.
Now I keep them in my pocket,
the right femur and the left femur.
Like a boy scout, I'm prepared.
For what can one say to a neighbour
when his wife dies? 'Sorry'?
Or when a friend's sweet child
suffers leukaemia? 'Condolences'?

No, if I should meet either friend
or stricken neighbour in the street
and he should tell me, whisper to me,
his woeful, intimate news,
wordless I take the two small femurs
from out of my pocket sadly
and play them like castanets.

May 9th

To reach Golders Green Tube station I need to pass a high brick wall situated near the corner of Rodborough Road and Finchley Road. It is unremarkable except there is a sign there, NO DUMPING. This morning I saw a bearded man standing before it and gesticulating. This was not Jerusalem and the man was not praying. On the contrary, he was pointing his index finger at the wall, wagging a finger at it in an accusatory manner. I was too far away to hear what he was saying. He seemed to be addressing the wall as if he were a vehement prosecuting attorney and that the brick wall had committed some misdemeanour.

As I approached he, becoming aware of me, stopped gesticulating, and stared down at the pavement as if he had dropped some minute object. At the corner of Finchley Road I glanced back and I could see he had recommenced his harangue at the culpable high brick wall. I walked on recalling how once I had heard an uncle of mine growling in the kitchen, 'You bastard. You're a real bastard. Oh you swine.' Alarmed I had walked in to discover he was talking to a drawer that would not open. He just said limply, 'It's jammed, Dannie.'

Talking to oneself of course does not necessarily signal a symptom of madness though this particular uncle of mine was somewhat eccentric. And what about all those caring women who, adding water to a vase, whisper to the flowers, 'There! Isn't that better?' I certainly soliloquise out loud much more now that I'm living alone. Having forgotten to switch off some electric appliance or when I have scalded a finger clumsily with some hot cooking utensil I hear myself saying, 'You idiot! You bloody fool!'

And on rare occasions I find my voice addressing Joan. 'You would have liked that', or 'I told you so'. I expect talking to one loved but dead is a common habit of the newly bereaved. I remember Canetti telling me about a widower in Vienna who at night, would whisper, to the portrait of her husband on the wall, 'Goodnight my love', then would *lick* it with passion before climbing the stairs to bed.

In *Fragments from my Diary* Gorky recollects a number of idiosyncratic behavioural incidents when a man believes himself to be alone. It seems Leo Tolstoy was overheard whispering to a lizard warming itself on a stone among the shrubs, 'Are you happy, eh?' Then after pondering for a moment, confided to the lizard, 'As for me, I'm not!'

Gorky reports how he watched a well-educated woman eating sweets in seeming solitude and addressing each of the candies which she held up in the air, 'I'll eat you up.'

'She was sitting at the time in an armchair at the window, at five o'clock on a summer's evening, and from the street the muffled noise of the big town filled the room. The face of this woman was serious, her greyish eyes fixed earnestly on the box of sweets in her lap . . .' when Gorky would hear her repeat again and again, 'I told you I'd eat you up, didn't I?'

I like, too, Gorky's anecdote about the priest, F. Vladimivsky, who one day placed a boot in front of him then commanded it to walk. He added, 'You see! You can't go anywhere without me.'

My own favourite voyeuristic experience of observing a person who believed she was unobserved occurred when I was a medical student lodging in a first floor room that overlooked the back garden of 38 Aberdare Gardens, Swiss Cottage. One of the other lodgers in that Victorian silent red-brick house was an old lady, a Mrs Schiff, a German-Jewish refugee who invariably dressed in black down to her ankles as if she were in mourning – which in fact she was because so many of her family had disappeared into the Nazi death camps. As I wrote in my autobiography, *Goodbye, Twentieth Century*:

One Sunday afternoon in 1943 I happened to turn towards my window and look down at the back garden below. On the lawn stood Mrs Schiff in her long black gown. She appeared shorter than the high sunflowers near the fence. Suddenly Mrs Schiff began to wave both her arms rhythmically. The old lady, not knowing she was being observed – perhaps listening to some symphony in her head – had begun to conduct an invisible orchestra. Waving her arms like that it seemed she wanted to take off from the lawn and fly. There were the sunflowers just moving perceptively in the wind, the apple tree full with its branches gently swaying, the grass, the one rosebush, the plants, the leaves, all obeying in slow movement the old grey-haired lady who was waving her arms about. I could see her distinctly smiling. She seemed so *happy*.

I turned away, thinking of her, thinking of from what she had escaped to conjure up blurred images from my ignorance. I remembered how, when I had first arrived in the house some ten months earlier, there had been a particularly noisy air-raid and we had filed down the stairs. Just after an explosion outside she had whispered a question: 'Mr Abse, please, are you a Jew?' . . . I returned to the window. On the lawn, Mrs Schiff had stopped conducting. She had her back to me, her round shoulders still. Then it occurred to me that Mrs Schiff had not been conducting inaudible music at all. She had been dancing to it. Dancing, in spirit, with her arms, dancing without moving her eighty-year-old feet. Dancing God knows when, in what year, what place, what world, and with whom I knew not, nor to which music.

When I think of Mrs Schiff standing on that back lawn now, though she was generally despondent, truly in mourning, I realise it was the temporary beneficent smile of happiness that made her pale wrinkled face lighten, to come alive. With common luck, most of those bereaved will experience such moments. I can vouch for it. And when I do discover, say, I'm humming quietly some favourite tune, I no longer tell myself I have no right to do so, but am glad for it, and am amazed.

May 13th

A week tomorrow I am to give a reading at Michael Joseph's café bookshop. Michael has invited Eleanor Bron to join me in reading poems from *Running Late*. The last time I performed at the bookshop was with Joan when we launched *Homage to Eros*, an anthology of love poems I edited. As I write now I have to suppress tear-provoking feelings for I can hear Joan's voice reading Anne Bradstreet's seventeenth-century poem addressed to her husband.

> If ever two were one, then surely we.
> If ever man were loved by his wife, then thee;
> If ever wife was happy in a man,
> Compare with me ye women if you can.
> I prize thy love more than whole mines of gold,
> Or all the riches that the East doth hold.
> My love is such that rivers cannot quench,
> Nor ought but love from thee, give recompense.
> Thy love is such I can no way repay.
> The heavens reward thee manifold I pray.
> Then while we live, in love let's so persever
> That when we live no more, we may live ever.

I do not know Eleanor Bron. When I spoke to her on the phone she told me that, like myself, she had lost her long-time partner. 'When?' I asked her. 'Three years ago,' she said. 'It doesn't get any better.'

She came here this morning to discuss what texts I would like her to read. Afterwards, inevitably, our dialogue veered towards the subject of bereavement. We managed to retain our composure but it was not difficult for me to see through the fenestra of Eleanor's words the turmoil of her feelings which indeed were like my own. I confessed to her, perhaps too tritely, how I found life somehow almost futile unless one could live purposefully for another person.

'I was able to do so. And now I can't,' I said.

'You're talking about love,' she said.

Eleanor Bron reminded me that we had both contributed to a BBC Radio 3 programme about language and how she had dwelt linguistically on what makes the world go round: love. After she left, I found amongst the books on my shelf a BBC publication called *More Words* and read in one of her contributions:

. . . though love as a concept is travestied and ridiculed and generally bandied about, as a word somehow it endures — vague and indestructible. Extraordinary claims are made for it — that it makes the world go round, for example, and absence of it fills the law courts and the psychiatrists' offices.

And the word 'love' is applied to all sorts of things

that at first sight may seem to have little or nothing in common. What is it about one's love of God, of work, country, parent, or of a favourite food, that is shared by purely sexual love or indeed unhappy and unsexual romantic love?

The nearest I can come to pinning it down, is that it is a drive to find something to which we can give priority, usually something outside ourselves against which to measure ourselves – which in fact gives us the echo that confirms our existence. So love is something that gives shape and order to our lives . . .

May 14th

Because of a promise I made almost twelve months ago, tomorrow I am to give a lecture at Hampstead Town Hall to the Third Age Association on how my experiences as a doctor have influenced my writings, particularly my poetry. I once delivered a similar lecture at Keats House in Hampstead entitled 'White Coat, Purple Coat' – white being the clinical colour while purple, metaphorically, refers to the mysterious, the poetical and the magical. (Didn't the Viennese physician and showman, Franz Anton Mesmer, wear his famous purple coat when he gazed deeply into his patients' eyes to 'mesmerise' them?) Indeed I once wrote a short poem about the difficulty of combining the two vocations:

> White coat and purple coat
>   a sleeve from both he sews.
> That white is always stained with blood,
>   that purple by the rose.

And phantom rose and blood most real
    compose a hybrid style;
white coat and purple coat
    few men can reconcile.

White coat and purple coat
    can each be worn in turn
but in the white a man will freeze
    and in the purple burn.

That difficulty has led many doctor-poets to eschew calling their medical experiences into their verse, among them John Keats, Robert Bridges, and for the most part too, even William Carlos Williams. For my part I have been pleased to take to heart Chekhov's response to the advice 'not to hunt after two hares'. He replied: 'I feel more confident and more satisfied with myself when I reflect that I have two professions and not one. Medicine is my lawful wife and literature is my mistress. When I get tired of one I spend the night with the other. Though it's disorderly, it's not dull, and besides, neither of them loses anything from my infidelity.'

Before the mid-1960s, like so many poet-doctors before me as far as poetry was concerned, I had been a fugitive from the traumatic incidents I had confronted while wearing a white coat. I had not taken advantage of being a privileged witness to patients' triumphs and defeats. Every patient has a story. On rare occasions the poet may, with the accidents of luck, exploit his craft and make entrance to it. I came to understand the relevance of Louis Pasteur's dictum, 'Chance favours

the prepared mind', and my mind, as it were, became
open, prepared to write poems coloured by my medical
experiences, and chance has favoured a number of such
poems over the years.

Tomorrow I shall refer during my lecture to these.
It will be strange to do so at Hampstead Town Hall,
for the last time I read poetry there was on Saturday,
February 4th 1961 when I had no thought of how
Apollo, the god of poetry, was also the father of
Aesculpius, the god of Medicine.

Then

That February Saturday evening I set out for
Hampstead Town Hall having been invited to read
there with Jon Silkin and Lydia Pasternak Slater, Boris
Pasternak's sister, by a young man I did not then
know, one named Jeremy Robson. I arrived somewhat
late to discover a long-winding queue and swirling
crowds on the Potemkin-like steps of the Town Hall
heaving towards the doors. Had I come on the wrong
night? Robson did say February 4th. 'Full up,' a man
was shouting at the Town Hall entrance. Perhaps I
had misheard the date? One would expect fifty people
or so to attend a poetry reading not hundreds. For
indeed hundreds were being turned away from the
Town Hall.

I struggled up through the crowd towards the front
doors which now were being closed by a burly citrine-
eyed man who chastised everyone who came near him,
'Full up, full up.' At last, confronting him, I said lamely,

half expecting to be contradicted, 'I'm one of the readers this evening.' He stared at me briefly as if I were some exotic zoo specimen. 'Full up,' he said, 'anyway it's started.' I slipped in while he was busy turning away a determined couple only to realise that I had surely made a mistake about the date, for from the high echoing chamber of the hall I could hear distinct jazz music and soon after a jocund voice saying, 'I thought tonight I would begin by reading you some sonnets by Shakespeare . . . but then I thought, why should I? He never reads any of mine.' The packed audience laughed and Spike Milligan, after reading comic verse, pointed at someone, 'You in the back, Yes, sir *you* . . . Oh sorry . . . madam!' It was with some relief that I recognised Jeremy Robson sitting next to Jon Silkin. Jeremy whispered something to Spike Milligan who then addressed the audience, 'Jeremy Robson tells me Dannie Abse has just come through the door. I wonder why he didn't open it?'

I'm afraid the proceedings at the Old Town Hall tomorrow, when I face the grey-haired audiences of The Third Age, will be altogether more sedate and predictable.

May 15th
After the lecture several of The Third Age audience came up to me to say a few hesitant words. One woman, elderly like all the others, told me her name as if I should know it: 'We met years ago in that coffee house in Swiss Cottage, the Cosmo,' she reminded me. 'You

look well. How's Joan?' And so once more – the larceny of my lotus contentment.

But I don't need such an importunate external reminder to lose equilibrium. I may be sitting in an armchair reasonably undisturbed, embedded in unstressful idleness, thinking about this or that, about inconsequential matters, or reading a book or listening to music or watching TV when suddenly I realise that Joan isn't upstairs in her study, nor in the kitchen preparing a meal, nor outside working in the garden, nor shopping, nor visiting an art gallery, and then I feel again the disquiet of her absences which makes me involuntarily cry out, 'Oh Joan!' I try to dam the impetuous gush of tears. And I think less than a year ago she did this, she did that, *it's not possible, it is not true.* But then I know it is true – and minutes pass, sometimes many minutes, before I resume to ponder about the usual inconsequential things, about this and that and where and when, and at what time. Else once more, on returning to a precarious contentment, I take up the book I had put aside or gaze at the far from sublime TV screen.

May 18th

In the current *London Review of Books* I learn that Alice Quinn, the poetry editor of the *New Yorker*, has edited the *Uncollected Poems, Drafts and Fragments* of that admirable American poet, Elizabeth Bishop. In her lifetime Bishop sanctioned only ninety poems from her four collections to be published in what she significantly called *Complete Poems*. It appears that for over a decade Alice Quinn sorted through 118 boxes containing some 3,500 pages of Elizabeth Bishop's papers in the Vassar College Library. So now, excluding the fragments, a further eighteen poems comprise her 'complete' *oeuvre*. The poet, herself, has been over-ruled.

Putting early manuscript material that poets during their lifetime may have rejected into the public domain is a thriving academic industry. Consequently, living poets can earn more money by selling their old work-sheets and workbooks to a university or a library than from the accumulated royalties received from all their published poetry books!

Yesterday, the academic critic, Professor A. T. Tolley, whom I've known for some years called on me. At present Trevor Tolley is here on a visit from his home in Ottawa. Last year Faber published Philip Larkin's *Early Poems and Juvenilia* which resulted from Tolley's scrupulous quixotic examination of the Larkin archive. Almost all of Larkin's discarded poems in this book are mediocre or transparent failures and those coming to Larkin for the first time might well not bother to investigate the poet's work further. So should a respected academic, however knowledgeable, however he may wish to honour the mature poet, pry into the poet's youthful manuscripts in order to edit and publish them?

Trevor Tolley argued, 'The high acclaim and exten-sive sales of Larkin's *Collected Poems* showed that he had become one of the most admired English poets of the twentieth century. His poems have indeed established themselves as among the major poetry of the period in English. His writings have been the subject of many studies and many learned gatherings, and his poems are part of the curricula of schools and universities. For these reasons alone, everything he wrote should be available to those who study his work; while everything he wrote is of interest to his admirers.'

'I'm not sure I would want my half a dozen admirers to focus on my rejected work. Or even on my earliest two published books,' I said.

'Where is your archive placed?' Trevor Tolley asked me.

My old manuscripts, workbooks, letters received, are collected in the National Library of Wales. Should I have destroyed them? Even as I impertinently ask myself that question I think how somewhere in Joan's study a bundle of my letters exist which I wrote to her over the decades while I was in the RAF or while travelling abroad on reading tours. I blundered on them once years ago. Also in that room, or elsewhere in the house, is a particular letter of mine which Joan hid, dating from the year 1949, and which, if I ever find it, will definitely be destroyed.

Then

In 1949, I, a medical student approaching my final examinations, lodged at 38 Aberdare Gardens, Swiss

Cottage. One morning I found on the front hall mat, an important-looking letter addressed to me from a library on the American east coast. Amazingly they knew that my first book of poems, *After Every Green Thing*, had been published recently, and with prodigious flattery asked if they might deposit the original manuscript of my book with all its corrections at their library so that present and future generations of scholars could learn from it.

Crikey! Posterity knocking on my door! I did not know that a similar letter had been sent at that time from this library to every newly published poet. Feeling very important I apologetically declined their request, blathering on at length about the complexity and mystery of the creative process. Years later, I realised how pompous and pretentious my response had been and I wished I had never written that letter – especially when one lunchtime, at the George pub, the BBC producer, John Gibson, remarked that probably the library had kept it in their files.

More years passed before an American librarian telephoned me.

'Dr Abse, I happen to be coming to London next week and I should like to meet you for lunch.'

'By all means, but why?'

'We, at the library, wonder whether you might have changed your mind about us having a manuscript of yours. We would value it greatly.' We made a deal. David Sorenson (not his real name) would return my jejune letter which indeed they had filed, in exchange for a few manuscript pages of a poem of mine. So some ten days later, at a table in the new Quality Inn, Tottenham Court Road, close to the chest clinic where I then worked, I sat opposite the elegantly dressed, manicured, cleaner-than-soap Mr Sorenson. Soon he extracted from an expensive-looking briefcase a large envelope. Clearing his throat, as if he was about to make a speech which would initiate a ceremony, he said earnestly, 'Here it is.' He held it up delicately as if it were a rare papyrus. 'It would be truly wonderful,' he continued, 'if you allowed us to keep your letter from the library as well as donating us the manuscript of a poem.'

'I'm sorry,' I said.

And so we exchanged 'documents' with suitable propriety and I immediately tore up the envelope and the letter, contained in it.

'No. My Gawd, no sir, you shouldn't have done that, no.'

I was startled by the vehemence of his protest. Across the table, above the glinting cutlery, I could see how his face had contorted into a nightmare horror – his former countenance revealed as a mere civilised mask. I felt a little guilty: I should have demolished the letter privately, not made such a dramatic gesture.

'YOU,' David Sorenson accused me, 'YOU have just destroyed a masterpiece.'

'Hardly.'

'Dr Abse you have destroyed a masterpiece,' he repeated. Again I stared across the table to see if he

had one eye closed. He seemed sure of his value judgement – indeed was irritatingly sober as if present at a
funeral.

When a year or so later Joan and I attended a function hosted by the Society of Authors we heard a discussion about American librarian interest in the manuscripts of British writers. When I mentioned to a
colleague that I had retrieved my letter, I was promptly
told, 'Dannie, they would have photostatted your letter
and kept the copy of it or even retained the original.'
(At that time photostatting in Britain was far from
commonplace.)

'Surely not,' Joan said, believing, as ever, people to
be trustworthy.

And I agreed with Joan, surely not, for I had witnessed
David Sorenson's agitated behaviour when I had torn
up the letter. Had he been extravagantly acting? Was
his, 'you have just destroyed a masterpiece' not simply
evidence of a ridiculous misjudgement, but that of
poker-faced foxery? Was I so naïve, so completely
beguiled?

In 1989, I think it was that year – as one gets older
a confusion of Time becomes such that Time past is
beyond Time – I had the opportunity to discover the
trustworthiness of Mr Sorenson for while on a reading
tour to promote a USA publication of one of my books
I had an invitation from an American professor to visit
the campus.

After my reading there the Professor of the English
Department fortunately introduced me to a large lady

with a youthful rose-lipped pretty face. She happened
to work at the library, and, better still she asked, 'Would
you care to see some manuscripts of your compatriots,
such as Edward Thomas or Dylan Thomas?'

Later that night she unlocked the doors of the library
and I in the cloistered silence followed her between the
stacks. As we ambled forward I asked, 'Does David
Sorenson still work here?'

'No,' she replied amiably. 'David left. He's in New
York now.'

I told her about my letter, about the agreement
Sorenson and I had fashioned together, and tentatively
raised the possibility of my letter having been photostatted.

'Of course not,' she smiled. 'We wouldn't do a thing
like that.'

After we peered solemnly at the Edward Thomas
manuscripts she, in order to reassure me opened the
metal cabinet which contained my sparse file. She
snapped it shut again and from the altered, now frac-
tious expression of her face I could see that my foolish
letter lived yet! Somewhere else, maybe in some desert,
480 leagues of demons and Lilith were laughing at me,
at my earlier naïvety.

'It's mine,' I demanded without enmity. 'We made a
bargain.'

'I can't give it you without consulting our chief
librarian,' she said. 'I'm sure he'll telephone you early
tomorrow morning.'

The call came and soon after 10 a.m. I sat in a significant conference room facing a half dozen people, all sitting in a row behind an imposing long polished horizontal table. The chief librarian apologised profusely, explained that there obviously had been a careless mistake and there had been no conspiratorial attempt to subvert the bargain agreed between myself and Mr Sorenson. He returned my letter, then hesitatingly beseeched, 'But we'd be delighted if you would donate more of your valued manuscripts to the care of our library, Dr Abse.' I declined his buttered invitation.

Outside the library the professor was waiting for me. 'What happened?' I showed him the letter. My aerial sense of being victorious was only momentarily brought to earth when the professor opined, 'They probably photostatted the photostat.' He smiled. 'No no, they wouldn't do that. We're all honourable men!'

Back home in London, after unpacking, I told Joan my story and held up the letter like a trophy. I was about to tear it up when Joan said, 'Well, let me read it first.' As far as I can recall I then needed to make some urgent telephone calls. Eventually when I asked Joan to return the letter she adamantly refused. 'The letter's OK. There's no need to destroy it.'

'Where is it?' I asked.

'I've hidden it,' she replied smiling.

'C'mon,' I said.

I was too tired to argue. I was jet-lagged. The bloody silly letter could wait for its certain annihilation. But more sovereign matters intervened. I forgot about it. So did Joan. Years later when the unimportant letter for some reason came to mind, Joan couldn't remember where she had hidden it.

May 20th

The hefty muscular gardener whom Joan employed occasionally last year came today. He is Portuguese and speaks little English. I observed him for a moment as he emerged from the bosky borders beyond the edge of the overlong grass. Mythic, he bent down towards the dark earth and dug into it sombrely as if it were the mysterious gateway to the underworld.

And I thought of inconsolable Orpheus, of his hopeless quest to defeat Thanatos, to bring his beloved from the inferno regions back home to this green, extraordinary, unfathomable living world that indisputably is, so that they could be together again in happy companionship. I imagined I heard faint voices as I stood there in the garden: Hermes saying, 'He has turned,' and a woman's half-comatose, thin, soft-sounding perplexed, 'Who?' as in Rilke's poem about Orpheus. And I thought how accurate that Who? for I know that relatives standing around the bed of a dying patient are poignantly dismayed when they realise they are not recognised by their loved one. Then I heard the gardener's voice but not what he said. I stared at his enquiring face.

Later

The gardener has long gone, but I've continued to think of the Orpheus myth. I've been wondering why widower

Orpheus was forbidden to look back. What a strange prohibition! What a strange taboo! Could that prohibition own a hidden sexual inference? Could the god's command, 'Do not look back' be reworded to 'Do not have sex with your wife'? In short, does the concealed meaning signal necrophilia?

Oh dear, I don't like that interpretation. I am vandalising a beautiful myth.

May 22nd

The launch of *Running Late* at the Michael Joseph bookshop restaurant went well enough. My own sanguinity became soluble when Eleanor Bron read two love poems addressed to Joan. Afterwards she chose two more poems from *Running Late*. Each had a sombre medical connotation. One about a Nigerian patient who believed he was possessed, the other about Alzheimer's disease. It was time to lighten matters and I hoped to cheer up myself as well as the audience by relating my part in a somewhat comical experience at an Uxbridge library many years ago.

Then

They had never organised a poetry reading at the library before. I was taken aback by my 'welcome'. At the door a stout woman sat behind a wooden table. 'Three pounds fifty,' she demanded.

'I'm ... er ... Dannie Abse,' I explained, noting behind her on the wall my name printed large on the poster announcement of the occasion.

'I don't care who you are,' she said. 'Three pounds fifty if you want to come to this poetry reading.'

'But I'm giving the reading.'

'What?'

'I'm Dannie Abse.'

'You're not the poet,' she said authoritatively.

'Yes,' I said.

She peered at me. I was being very closely examined. Worse, an impatient queue was forming behind me, one of whom seemed a little tipsy.

'Go on,' the stout lady jeered. 'You look ordinary.'

'Look –' I began.

'You look ordinary,' she announced happily, 'I could cuddle you.'

'Let the bugger in,' shouted the tipsy man behind me.

This was very different from the welcome I received at the Cambridge International Poetry Festival. Then, when I arrived, I heard people say excitedly, 'Dannie Abse's here, Dannie Abse's here,' and I was surprised and warmed by their apparent delight at my arrival. As I moved through the corridor to the reception centre, again the murmuring, 'He's here, he's here.' This is the best welcome I've ever had, I thought. When I finally reached reception one of the organisers sprang to her feet as if I was the Messiah at last manifest. 'Oh Dannie Abse, I'm so pleased you're here,' she said. 'Thank God, we're desperate. Could you please write a prescription for one of the Greek poets who has a terribly painful gum infection and is due to read here tomorrow.'

The chairs in the Uxbridge library gradually became occupied. Soon the far from urbane chairman introduced me and complimented the valiant audience for bothering to turn up for a mere poetry reading on such a pleasant June evening. I had not read and chatted for more than five minutes before there was an untamed disturbance at the back. I could not see what was happening but three men appeared to be wrestling with each other before, suddenly, a door slammed and the unwelcome cacophony subsided. I then read to an attentive audience. Some time later I became aware of a figure standing on the pavement outside. He leant towards one of the half-open library windows and remained there, statuesque, listening to my reading. After a further five minutes or so I walked to the window and invited him to come inside and take a seat.

'Can't,' he shouted. 'They threw me out. I'm pissed.'

May 23rd

Susanna tells me the inquest is to take place next month. I hope I won't have to attend. Nowadays I don't often conjure up the scene of the car accident but I still avoid driving any distance. Even as a car passenger I am too tense, too alert.

I drove over to Hampstead last night to be at a dinner party given by Ed and Brita Wolf whom I hardly know. Afterwards, back home, I felt pleased with myself simply because I had not made the journey by bus. Ridiculously pleased — as if I had jumped over a chasm of gathering darkness where snakes writhed below! Wonderful bold me!

When I think of the accident, only latterly have I realised how eerie it is that on 13th last June I crawled out of that capsized, concertinaed car without any vexed, enduring physical handicap. After leaving hospital I reflected early on that I might have been killed outright. That would have been OK. I would not have known that Joan had suffered the same terminal fate. But perhaps because of brief bouts of self-pity I have been in partial denial about how fortunate I am – I could easily have been crippled, blinded, or brain damaged. So I should and do count the alphabet of my blessings and affirm that the words, 'yes' and 'thank you' are amongst the most beautiful of our language. Yet whom does one thank? All the thanksgiving prayers are null and void for one secular such as myself. At best I can assent to the Greek poet who wrote:

> Speak, almond tree.
> Speak to me of God
> Behold, the almond blossomed.

At Ed Wolf's dinner party I sat next to Jenny, a widow, who obviously had been primed of the car accident and its consequences. She declared that she found vital solace in chatting about her husband. 'Most widows like to do that don't they? My husband has been dead for four years,' she continued, confidentially, 'I still write a letter to him every day.' She touched the sleeve of my arm sympathetically. 'I feel most comfortable, most at ease with those who know the stressed experiences of bereavement.'

I declined to talk to this stranger, pleasant woman though she was, about Joan. Why should I reveal to her how utterly caring Joan was; her feminine sweetness and gullibility; her patience with fools; how, unlike her husband, she never boasted of her accomplishments! I doubt I'd experience 'vital solace' by telling Jenny of Joan's interest in the history of work; how she loved listening to abstract arguments about politics, aesthetics, ethics, anything; how she enjoyed swimming, always daring to go further from the shore than I thought wise. (At Pesaro, one summer holiday, we both nearly drowned.) What was it to one such as Jenny, a stranger, that Joan, when a schoolgirl, improbably played Jaques in *As You Like It* or had a poem published in a national Sunday newspaper when she was but eight years old? That she engaged in all pleasurable activities with relish — did so with a passionate concentration whether researching a book, or gardening, or visiting an art gallery, or making monogamous love.

May 26th

They fear a summer drought but this evening it rains as it frequently has done for a week or so now. From this window I can view the front garden and count three dandelions, little lanterns startling the darkening overgrown grass. Soon the rain will drag the night down and the rain will become visible only as it slants across the lit lamp posts of urban Hodford Road. Now it's still daytime rain, so delicate and thin that it seems ashamed to be seen except where it pricks a pool on the concrete road. It is the sort of rain that makes the smudge of evening feel curiously familiar, as if it has arrived like a gloomy echo of an evening from another decade, another year, from a time long past and forgotten.

Now an early light comes on in the windows of a house across the road and, immediately, the whole street becomes darker ... I'm alone, I mean I'm not merely alone but suddenly, with that light coming on, I've become aware that I am alone. Occasional cars, some with headlights on intermittently swish by saying 'Hush'.

May 30th
This morning's newspapers about the recurring decimal of calamity in Iraq (Troops hit by roadside bomb on patrol in Basra; TV crew caught up in attack on US convoy) reminds me that Tony Curtis is putting together an anthology of anti-war texts by Welsh authors. I wish he would include a poem of mine called 'The Victim of Aulis', despite its occasional linguistic lapses. It is probably too long anyway for the limited space Tony is allowed; besides it's ostensibly about an incident during the distant Trojan War. In that, it resembles the best anti-war poem since 1918,

one written by the Greek poet, George Seferis. The epigraph to his poem is taken from Euripides' play, *Helena* which says it all:

Helena: I never went to Troy. Only a phantom went.
Messenger: What? All that suffering for nothing?

Euripides offered the alternative legend of Helen's absence from Greece. She was in Cyprus, not with Paris at Troy. I imagine Paris kissing a pillow where Helen was not, straddling the phantom he thought he saw and, soiling the sheets, lying back still jerking, 'Helen, Helen,' satisfied. Meanwhile, the Greeks and Trojans were murdering each other and they continued to do so for ten long years. 'All,' as Seferis writes, 'for a linen garment, a phantom made of air, a butterfly's flicker, a wisp of a swan's down, an empty tunic — all for a Helen.'

In our time Bush and Blair have replaced the name Helen with three intials: WMD. And tens of thousands of Iraqi civilians, thousands of US and Iraqi troops, and many of our soldiers number among the slaughtered dead.

Then

It must have been 1953 and a slow London summer's evening. I had left the clinic where I worked at Cleveland Street (across the road from the Middlesex Hospital) and was walking past the Fitzroy pub in Charlotte Street when I was accosted by a well-built rosy-faced man with a pronounced Irish accent. 'Excuse me,' he said. 'You're Dannie Abse, right? You know Paul Potts.'

'Yes,' I answered.

'I hope you don't mind at all but I bought a magazine, *Stand*, the other day with your name on the cover. You had a pome in it. I read de pome called "The Victim of Something or other".'

'The Victim of Aulis'

'I read de pome up, I read it down, I read it sideways but I couldn't understand the bloody ting. It was opaque to me entirely.'

'If you know the myth you wouldn't find it difficult.'

'Sure I know lots of myths but I don't happen to know this particular one.' He must have sensed my impatience because he said, 'I'll walk wid yer and you can tell me.'

We progressed towards Rathbone Place. I had no choice. 'Well, you know about the Trojan War, how the Greeks sailed to Troy?'

'Sure, it was a desperate time.'

'On the way to Troy, the sailing boats carrying the Greek legions were stuck for days in the harbour of Aulis because there was no wind.'

'No wind,' the Irishman repeated,

'So the priest, Calchas, advised King Agamemnon, that the wind would arise only if he, the king, sacrificed his young daughter.'

My new Irish acquaintance stopped walking. We were

now in Rathbone Place. His sanguineous face seemed troubled. 'Sacrifice his daughter, sacrifice his own daughter – to whom?'

'To Artemis,' I said.

He nodded. 'Yes,' he snorted suddenly, 'I lost three quid on that fucker last week.'

I laughed. It was a mistake. He was not joking. 'Give my regards to Paul Potts if you see him,' I said. I left him there, hesitant, outside the Wheatsheaf pub in Rathbone Place. I don't remember where I was going to. Why that direction? It was summer. It was 1953. Joan would have been pregnant with our first daughter, Keren, and I was happy.

May 31st
It is almost four o'clock in the morning, still dark. I woke up a couple of hours ago and couldn't go back to sleep so came downstairs to make myself a cup of tea. It is very quiet. I hear my pen moving across this paper!

I think of Q who wrote a letter to me last week. I should answer her and write other letters that I also owe rather than attending to this journal. It's just as well Q is in New York. This moment I would welcome physical contact, the warmth of another living being. Women come to mind: friends whom I have known over the years. Inevitably they were friends of Joan too. Many of these are now divorcees or widows, almost as old as myself, and perhaps lonely. I like and admire a number of them and wish I could be attracted in a physical way to one or another of them. But I'm not. Their eyes, steady, are friendly.

I looked up just now and saw (can see) some purple irises Leony, the Filipino girl who cleans the house, must have picked from the garden, and Coleridge's line from his Dejection Ode 'I see, not feel, how beautiful they are' comes home to me not for the first time latterly.

June 1st

In the voluminous main space of Golders Green Library next to a notice, PLEASE DON'T LEAVE YOUR BAGS UNATTENDED, I sat at one of the grey plastic-top tables reading the current issue of the *TLS*. Soon I became aware of a half-suppressed hostile argument conducted in a foreign language (Polish?) between the man and the woman occupying one of the neighbouring tables.

A library is supposed to be a quiet place and evidently the couple were conscious of my glances as they lowered their voices to an urgent whisper. I tried to resume reading the *TLS* but suddenly their voices explosively erupted and the woman stood up. Then she darted out of the library. The man turned to me and said in perfect English, 'My wife was being unreasonable.' Five minutes or so later he, too, quit the library and I sat back for a moment looking up at the very high ceiling to observe how one of the long tubes of neon light was on a vibrant blink.

Walking back home I thought of the tiffs that I had with Joan over the decades. I was surprised that I could recall few specific rows and not one of their causes. Once Joan tried in exasperation to hit me and I had to hold on firmly to her wrists. What was all that about? What had I done or not done? Probably I had been insensitive about something or other and maybe, *maybe*, she had been unreasonable!

Another occasion, one midnight, I had become so furious with Joan, so incensed about something now long forgotten — what hurtful words had been uttered? what vanity mortified? — that I, boiled in self-righteous anger, stamped vehemently out of the house as if for ever. I remember sitting in our car (it would have been a Morris Minor). Probably I lit a cigarette since, in those days, I used to smoke despite working in a chest clinic. I don't think I hesitated too long before driving away into the glum darkness of infinity.

That Friday night, at that hour, there would have been little traffic and it seemed to me no time at all before I realised I was approaching the village of Barnet. I did not know anybody in Barnet. Besides, even if I did, it would be too late to call on anybody. In the embers of my temper, I decided there was not much I could do except turn the Morris Minor around, head for the Finchley Road, and southwards go home. It was either that or sleeping in the car. I was suddenly feeling very, very tired. In ignoble retreat, a quarter of an hour later, I observed the clock-tower monument of Golders Green in front of me.

Joan, surely now, would be asleep, oblivious, in our bedroom. Driving, I parked the car. Hodford Road seemed particularly empty because of its sentinel lamp posts but, unlike the dark houses of our neighbours, a welcoming light illuminated the curtains of our upstairs bedroom. May that Polish (?) couple I encountered today at Golders Green Library, whatever the aetiology of their disputation, discover as I did, the secret sweet armistice of the double bed.

June 2nd

Lazy morning. Though awake I stay in bed late. How does the song go: 'Lazy bones, lying in the sun.' The summer sun arrived ostentatiously in Golders Green this morning. Women walk by in flimsy dresses, the postman wears shorts. And I decide to breakfast at the open-air café in Golders Hill Park.

On the sloping grass that rises from the path which skirts the pond a little girl in a pink T-shirt was talking to a worried-looking duck that had settled there. The child's mother busily continued gossiping with her companion. I slowed my pace near the rhapsody of purple azaleas as I observed the child begin to chase the duck that had hopped away. When the duck, alarmed, flew off the little girl opened her arms wide as if she too wished to fly. She rushed down the slope arms still extended until she tumbled just before she reached the path. Immediately the child began to cry. Such a weeping. But was it because she had physically hurt herself or because she could not catch her desired duck or because she could not fly?

The young mother picked up the child to console

her. 'Where does it hurt?' I heard her say. And I wondered whether the little girl would point to the region of her heart! 'Come, tell me,' said the mother, 'I'll kiss it better.' I walked on thinking how she had said 'I'll kiss it better' and how love sometimes can heal. Then I recalled a poem I had read many years ago by the American poet, Peter Viereck:

Of Course Not

The happiest landscape my eyes ever meddled
    with —
Pines, waterfall, and a most stately lawn —
Is the view they call Paradise Pond in Northampton
    at Smith
Then comes a hedge, and a hospital further on.

My boy of three was watching me watch this
    view
When I learnt once more how ambiguous
    everything is.
He, too, had his dogmas; he 'knows' for a fact it is
    true
That a hurt goes away with a kiss.

My eyes were so full of Paradise Pond I agreed
With my son for an instant as slim as the hedge
    that hides
'Mass. State Hospital', crammed inside
With the crazy and the hurt. Is it lack of a kiss
Made the State of Mass. need a house like this?
Of course not. Or, come to think of it, yes indeed.

Then

I had come down the stairs of our first floor Belsize Park flat to respond to a desperately insistent bell being rung. I opened the front door to discover a tall trembling figure whom I had met but once, briefly, at the Greyhound pub in Dulwich. It was David Gascoyne. In 1954 David Gascoyne was a much respected poet and translator whose most recent book had been illustrated by Graham Sutherland.

Before I could say a word he, 'wild of eye', agitated, began to babble, 'I'm being pursued by a Pole. Ever since I left the midwifery hospital he's been following me.'

'Midwifery hospital?'

I searched his haunted, rather handsome face.

'They locked me up there in a padded cell. I escaped. Please let me in. Please please please.'

I hesitated. That summer evening my mother happened to visit me from Cardiff in order to see us both and to cuddle our baby, Keren. They were upstairs, Joan and my mother at the table, having just finished dinner. Keren was in her cot.

'He chased me all the way,' David Gascoyne continued desperately. 'That Pole can't be far. He can't be far.'

'You better come in,' I said.

Upstairs I introduced him to Joan and my mother. He ignored them. Addressing me he commanded, 'Ring Biddy Crozier, ring Biddy Crozier, tell her I'm besieged.' Then his language became confused and not at all under the control of reason. He could have been one who helped build the Tower of Babel.

'Come and have something to eat, David,' my mother said firmly.

I did not know whether David had swallowed too many amphetamines or whether I was witnessing a schizoid delirium. He certainly needed nursing care. Biddy Crozier? I had heard that name somewhere. As David Gascoyne babbled and trembled I looked up the name Biddy Crozier in the directory. When I did speak to her and related how David Gascoyne needed urgent attention Biddy Crozier asked for my address. 'You're not too far away,' she said. 'I won't be long. Tell David I'm coming. I'll come at once.'

One afternoon more than a decade later, my cousin Michael Shepherd who worked with Aubrey Lewis at the Maudsley Hospital, asked me if I had ever heard of a poet called David Gascoyne.

'Yes, of course. Why do you ask?'

'He's in a catatonic state. He's been moved from hospital to hospital. He's mute. He doesn't speak at all. I believe he once wrote some rather fine religious poetry.'

'Yes, he did. He hasn't published anything for years. I suppose he's been too ill. Alas. I'm sorry.'

I envisioned David Gascoyne older, silent, petrified. Much of his published poetry had always suggested it was by one who had suffered.

In the late spring of 1979, startled, I received a letter from the Isle of Wight inviting me to give a reading in Cowes at the request of David Gascoyne who would be my chair. The secretary of the local poetry society added that some time in October would be most suitable. I was curious of course. I accepted the invitation.

I expected David Gascoyne would look older. A quarter of a century had passed since his spectacular entrance to our flat in Belsize Park; but I was nevertheless shocked when he came towards me with outstretched hand. He was now pendently tall, anorexically thin, a figure for Giacometti to sculpt. His voice, a little tremulous said, 'Dannie, when I saw you last I was not too well.' I was surprised he remembered the occasion. 'I was not well during my forties. I was not well during my fifties. But now in my sixties, I'm OK.'

I learnt how he had been cured. His new wife, Judy, was pleased to tell me — indeed she was to inform all acquaintances of David as well as strangers — of how one morning she visited the Isle of Wight Mental Hospital to read poetry to some of the patients. When at one point she said, 'That poem was by David Gascoyne,' a hollow earnest voice from the back of the room announced, 'I AM HE,' she assumed the tall damaged man who had made the claim was deluded.

Judy, afterwards, mentioned the incident to the superintendent of the hospital who assured her that the patient was indeed David Gascoyne and that he was taken aback that Gascoyne had at last broken his prolonged silence.

Subsequently Judy visited David at the hospital regularly, and because of her natural warmth and her evident admiration of his work, he gradually responded, recovering from his slatternly inertia, to speak more and more. After months of such saviorous care and attention she was allowed to nurse David at her home. They fell in love. 'And now he's well and we're married,' Judy Gascoyne rejoiced.

Years passed and David began publishing occasional translations again. He died in November 2001. Not one of the successive psychiatrists had cured David Gascoyne. Not one of the prescribed drugs. Nor any other therapy. Judy, though, had kissed him better. Triumphantly.

June 4th

When I visited Dr Meehan on February 4th and declined to be his patient, he sympathetically remarked, 'Should you change your mind, I shall be here. I think you should come if your symptoms persist.'

There has been some abatement of these symptoms but they still persist. For instance, I'm emotionally labile and too often the lit candle goes out. I may drive the car more, say to Muswell Hill to dine with Paul and Susanna, but when I do, the alert adrenaline flows. And I'm not yet ready to return to Ogmore or travel any distance that would require me to stay in an hotel for a night. I ridiculously need my nest. Even so, I'm not inclined to sit and disgorge egrimony facing the psychiatrist's chair.

In one of the gnostic gospels found in December

1945, at a cave near the upper Egyptian town of Nag Hammandi, Jesus is reported to have riddled, 'If you bring forth what is within you, what you bring forth will save you. If you do not bring forth what is within you, what you do not bring forth will destroy you.' Elaine Pagels, a professor of religion at Princeton University, quotes that admonition in her book *The Gnostic Gospels* which I am, at present, reading. She finds it a cryptic remark as well as one that is compelling. It seems like wise psychoanalytical advice to me. One doesn't have to be a penitent Christian to heed it or believe in Satan and the demiurge.

I wonder how Wilfred would have reacted to the above paragraphs. He believed that psychoanalysis was not only a healing process but a wonderful form of education. ('Wonderful' was one of Wilfred's favourite words. 'Would you like a second helping, Wilf?' 'Yes, wonderful.' 'Can I drive you into Cardiff?' 'Wonderful. Thank you.') I miss Wilfred very much, my good-natured brother who, like Joan would always think the best of people. He often talked about moving back to South Wales after retirement to live in the place he loved – Ogmore, but his wife, Elizabeth was not keen.

Wilfred was such a family man. When he and Elizabeth were holidaying this side of the Atlantic for a few weeks he, much to Elizabeth's irritation, would spend long hours with all the many uncles, aunts, and cousins, scattered in the county of Glamorgan. No wonder before falling ill Wilfred was working on a book provisionally entitled, *The Sense of Belonging*.

When I was a boy he was the one to whom I would turn for advice. He would listen with insightful patience. If he were alive and well I would turn to him now, though there is a hurt no doctor or kiss can heal.

June 6th

Not yet six o'clock in the morning, the sunlight must have wrenched me from sleep and only half awake, disordered, I found myself crying. The previous night I had not drawn the curtains properly and I had blinked my eyes open to see Joan's photograph on the shelf opposite me. That photograph is there permanently. It does not usually signal frank tears. When I managed to cease sniffing I thought of Thomas Hardy's lines about his dead wife: 'Where you will next be there's no knowing/ Facing round about me everywhere.' And before I took breakfast I went to the bookshelves and read Hardy's whole poignant poem which he wrote in 1912.

After a Journey

Hereto I come to view a voiceless ghost;
    Whither, O whither will its whim now draw me?
Up the cliff, down, till I'm lonely, lost,
    And the unseen waters' ejaculations awe me.
Where will you next be there's no knowing,
    Facing round about me everywhere,
      With your nut-coloured hair,
And grey eyes, and rose-flush coming and going.

Yes: I have re-entered your olden haunts at last;
    Through the years, through the dead scenes I
    have tracked you;
What have you found now to say of our past –
    Scanned across the dark space wherein I have
    lacked you?
Summer gave us sweets but autumn wrought
    division?
        Things were not lastly as firstly well
            With us twain, you tell?
But all's closed now, despite Time's derision.

I see what you are doing: you are leading me on
    To the spots we knew when we haunted here
    together,
The waterfall, above which the mist-bow shone
    At the then fair hour in the then fair weather,
And the cave just under, with a voice still so hollow
    That it seems to call out to me from forty years
    ago,
        When you were all aglow,
And not the thin ghost that I now fraily follow!

Ignorant of what there is flitting here to see,
    The waked birds preen and the seals flop lazily,
Soon you will have, Dear, to vanish from me,
    For the stars close their shutters and the dawn
    whitens hazily.
Trust me, I mind not, though Life lours,
    The bringing me here; nay bring me here again!
        I am just the same as when
Our days were a joy, and our path through flowers.

June 7th

I met my literary agent, Robert Kirby, today at the Pizza Express in Coptic Street near the British Museum as I have done every couple of months or so for decades. He suggests that I let him have this manuscript after he returns from his holiday in July so that he can advise me whether it could and should be published or not. Was Nietzsche right or merely cynical when he averred that 'one writes books in order to conceal what is concealed in one'?

For some time I have had, as my imaginary readers, Keren, Susanna and David. They know I've been writing this journal/memoir/anthology and have encouraged me to do so. I hope if this manuscript does get published they will consider it not merely as a Look-at-Me insolent journal but one that is a salute to their virtuous mother. Now, though, it is disturbing for me to entertain the idea of closure.

'I couldn't make it more cheerful, more varnished,' I warned Robert.

'Of course, I understand. There is no happy ending.'

'I don't know what I'll do each morning if I don't apply myself to write about the woeful Now and the happier Then.'

'You'll start another book,' said Robert with alarming confidence.

I try to imagine myself as a vigilant reader of the manuscript, one who is neither a relative nor a sympathetic acquaintance but a cool stranger. Would it engage his or her interest? Many of the poems I quote are not testaments of joy. As my friend, the American critic, M. L. Rosenthal, used to drily say, 'There's something about a funeral that depresses me!' On the other hand, should that reader be a new or old widow or widower, one left abruptly not so much in darkness but in a different place and alone as never before, then perhaps the book, like a radio playing in a distant room, may provide at least some frail consoling company. I would like to think so.

June 9th

The movable flower stall, at the corner where Hodford Road meets the main Golders Green Road, only makes its appearance nowadays on a Friday. The ageing proprietors, a man and a woman (husband and wife?) are presumably in semi-retirement. They have sold flowers there for as long as I can remember. I am familiar to them because, over the decades, I used to buy freesias for Joan. The couple must have been puzzled when I ceased to do so, passing by only to exchange faint smiles.

I guess that the stall appears on Fridays because the many orthodox Jews of the neighbourhood buy celebratory flowers for their wives on the Sabbath eve. (Aren't religious Jews encouraged to make love to their wives especially on a Friday night?) 'He who is without a wife,' the Talmud proclaims, 'dwells without blessing, life, joy, help, good, and peace.'

Anyway, this Friday morning, on reaching the corner stall, I noted that among the variety of flowers on display were some tall unopened red gladioli. 'Yes,' the woman said. 'It's early. These are Dutch gladioli.' I did not buy them but I recalled another occasion two years ago when I did so, and presented Joan with a poem.

With Compliments

Dear, if I had a small legacy from Croesus
I would purchase – please do not argue –
that painting of gladioli by Soutine
you so admired. But in a waking fit
of realism I've bought
this bunch of true, robust-red
radiantly alive upstanding gladioli
from the Corner Flower Stall instead.

Then

Long before I bought those gladioli I happened to be just quitting the corner flower stall carrying a bunch of white freesias (I don't believe it was necessarily a Friday!) when a familiar voice mocked, 'I hope those are for Joan.' I turned to a grinning Sigi Nissel. I probably quipped something like, 'No, these are for Queen Elizabeth.' One tended to be light-heartedly jocular in the presence of benign Sigi Nissel.

Sigi, the Amadeus Quartet's second violinist, like many a musician, was always eager to tell one a joke. And as we lingered beside the flower stall he was soon doing so – alluding to a certain Mrs Hetti Cohen whose husband had just died. According to Sigi she had put a notice in the local paper: ABE COHEN DEAD. Mrs Cohen was then informed that for the same money she could add more words. Sigi continued, 'Hetti Cohen pondered. After significant contemplation she pronounced, 'OK. Thank you. ABE COHEN DEAD. VOLVO FOR SALE.'

When I presented Joan with the freesias I repeated Sigi Nissel's joke. It genuinely amused her. Neither of us tended to be joke-tellers. (The trouble about telling someone a joke is that you will have to listen to three more.) Besides, after a short time, Joan and I disremembered them. Sigi's joke was, for some unknown reason, an exception. It became Joan's one joke though she was always reluctant to render it. But on the rare social occasions where it was appropriate I would encourage her to do so, because, afterwards, she would laugh as much as her auditors and I enjoyed seeing her so mirthly animated and happy.

June 10th
One of my neighbours is very much aware that I was trained as a doctor. He always inadvertently emphasises the word 'doctor' when he addresses me. And if there happens to be current news about likely medical disasters such as bird-flu or about nutritional health (British kids are much too fat, *doctor*) he is eager to engage me in conversation should I meet him in the precincts of Golders Green. I believe that he has such an old-fashioned attitude about the prestigious status of doctors that if it were fashionable to wear a hat

he would cautiously raise it whenever he passed my gate.

So this morning when he greeted me as I left Barclays Bank in Finchley Road I was surprised that his prattle was free of medical references. On the contrary, he diverted the conversation towards poetry. He evidently had seen my book *Running Late* on the shelf at Waterstones in Hampstead. (Seen it, not bought it!) Perhaps it was the proximity of Barclays Bank that prompted him to say sympathetically, 'Can't be much in writing poetry, *doctor*.' He looked at me, puzzled. I had the feeling that I had gone down in his estimation. Perhaps not. But before I managed to escape I had the distinct impression that, in future, when he calls me 'doctor', it will not be in italics.

Then

Poets are not high earners. On the contrary. In some quarters, though, their status is higher than that of physicians. So, from time to time they are granted privileges such as the one I experienced in Cardiff some years ago.

It was mid-afternoon. I had visited a friend who lived near Roath Park Lake. Ten minutes later, approaching Ninian Road that faces the Recreation Ground I became aware that I needed to pee, keenly and increasingly aware with each minute that passed. Then I recalled that when a schoolboy I played football the other side of these railings that enclosed the recreation ground and that there used to be a public urinal at its far Penylan end.

Already I could see its structure in the distance and increased my pace. Reaching the urinal though, I was amazed to read its notice: FOR WOMEN ONLY. Wales is a matriarchal society where Mam is Queen and King but this, I felt, was absurd. Why weren't men allowed to micturate there? Maybe there was a story in the *South Wales Echo* which would explain it all. Men behaving badly, perhaps? Anyway my need was now acutely urgent.

Fortunately, nearby, I could see a prefabricated one-storey building which turned out to be a local library. Surely they would have a lavatory there? Soon after I opened the front library door I confronted a pensive man behind a counter, engaged in stamping books. He glanced up, eyebrows raised, when I asked, 'Excuse me, have you a loo here?' He stopped stamping the books. Then seeming to ignore the question he resumed thumping the books energetically, thud, thud, thud. At last he raised his head again to scrutinise me. 'It's private, for the staff only,' he said. Then, hesitating, he added, 'Ah, but we allow poets to use it.'

Such privileges we poets have. We can have a piss in a Cardiff library free!

Now, as I write this, I recall the poem the American poet, Dabney Stuart, wrote about his son. He gave it the witty title '*Sunburst*'.

> A friend writes
> *How's the prince?*
> *I bet he's a pisser.*

He is.
Anywhere:
In his bath
Naked under the sun
Getting his pants changed
The sudden burst
The rise
The high peak
And the fall.

Not a word
But this bow
Warm as spring rain
Rainbow
Pot of Gold
Dazzling
Curve of the world.

When he grows up
May he find
Such light
Such shape
Such perfect levity
For what he can't use.

June 11th

Despite the wettest May for twenty-seven years ground
water levels are reported to be dangerously low so, now
that we are in the middle of a heatwave, hosepipes have
been banned. A possible summer drought is feared. Our
back garden which Joan attended to so diligently looks
thirsty this Sunday morning. I was up early, so before

the sun entirely cleared the rooftops of our house, with the garden in part shadow, I filled watering cans and did my duty for half an hour. Then, bored, I rewarded myself by resting on the old wooden bench under the very old, geriatric apple tree. Surprisingly, I heard no bird song. Were the abundant wood pigeons, the magpies, the young chaffinches I observed through the kitchen window a week ago all anaesthetised by the heat? The tall dark green trees, windless, whispered no answer.

I wished it would thunder, June thunder, and drench the fissured earth, and all those roses which this year wear their colours extravagantly: bold blatant red; the deeper crimson ones close to the now fading blue irises; the yellow lemon roses and the white, the white as thickly rich as cream is. There are so many flowers in the garden I've never seen before, plants that Joan must have seeded, they are nameless to me. They all need water.

As I sat on the wooden bench a solitary white butterfly floated over the bushes near the wall and I recalled the note I had written among the aphorisms in my note book: 'Should you see a white butterfly, little solitary soul, staggering in a churchyard, rising above stone tablets, then stumbling, then rising again, like one learning how to fly, have the grace to stand still for a moment.'

The garden was no churchyard but I stood up till the butterfly vanished, then went back into the house.

Then

We moved into our Ogmore house, 'Green Hollows' in 1972. Our garden there, thanks to Joan's industry, became truly handsome despite the bruised purple-red valerian known locally as Devil's Dung that, weed-like, would spring up right, left and centre.

When Leo and his wife, Marjorie, visited us Marjorie became much interested in an important-looking tree near our wooden six-bar gate. She plucked a leaf from it. 'It has a medicinal odour,' she said puzzled. 'What kind of tree is it?' We didn't know. Marjorie knew an expert who worked at Duffryn Gardens. 'He'll know,' Marjorie said confidently. 'I'll show him this leaf.'

Later we learnt that the tree that had a whiff of a dispensary about it was, according to Marjorie's expert a rare Korean tree, an Evodia Danieli. 'I like the name Danieli,' I told Joan. Afterwards, visitors were invited to pluck a leaf and have a sniff of our *rare* Oriental tree. Indeed I boasted about that tree as if I had planted it. Then came the drought of 1976. That summer, to our astonishment, in an existentialist fury the tree revealed its true identity. 'Look, look up there,' Joan commanded me. 'Those are some sort of nuts.'

'Rare Evodia Danieli nuts,' I said. 'It's the hot weather.'

We managed to bring a couple down. Joan peeled them. Then opened one to expose a small brain-like walnut.

'It's just a walnut tree,' Joan said.

'A *Korean* walnut tree?' I suggested.

June 12th
An uncomfortable, hot London day. Tomorrow it will be exactly a year since the accident and I still don't

know the date for the inquest. Cary Archard is visiting London on Wednesday and has asked if I could put him up for the night. I think how he admired Joan as a writer. In the *New Welsh Review* he wrote, 'Would it be fair to say that Joan belonged to that generation of women who put their family first? I'm not sure how useful such a generalisation is. I could suggest that most of these women might have wanted their lives to be something else – something that certainly would not be true in Joan's case. Nevertheless, when I look at her publications, I wish that she had given us more. Her biography of Ruskin is a remarkable achievement, scholarly (she seemed to have read everything by that prolific writer) and readable, without ever losing control of the multifarious strands of Ruskin's life . . .'

Maybe that's what I should do next. Instead of sitting here at this desk I could linger in the estrangement of Joan's study (overlooked by the portrait of Ruskin on the mantelpiece) and examine all those unfinished manuscripts of hers that I know fill the desk's drawers. (For a whole year I've hardly entered this upstairs room.) Yet I might miss, not only for my health's sake, continuing with these entries. For doing so has allowed me sometimes the pleasure of escaping into a benign Past. The Past, indeed, can sometimes be a sanctuary.

June 13th
I believed an aeroplane, possibly in difficulties, flew much too low over our house. The fusillades of

growling near noise became louder and prodigiously louder. I was alarmed that the plane would crash against and into our roof, and I woke up abruptly. The dream did not require a Daniel to be deciphered, especially as it is exactly one year ago that I lost, in one unpredictable moment, my lover, my ally, and my friend. As Robert said, 'There is no happy ending.'

Lachrymae

(i) Later

I went to her funeral.
I cried.
I went home that was not home.

What happened cannot keep.
Already there's a perceptible change of light.
Put out that light. Shades
lengthen in the losing sun.
She is everywhere and nowhere
now that I am less than one.

Most days leave no visiting cards behind
and still consoling letters make me weep.
I must wait for pigeon memory
to fly away, come back changed
to inhabit aching somnolence
and disguising sleep.

(ii) Winter

What is more intimate
than a lover's demure whisper?
Like the moment before Klimt's *The Kiss*.
What's more conspiratorial
than two people in love?

So it was all our eager summers
but now the yellow leaf has fallen
and the old rooted happiness
plucked out. Must I rejoice when
teardrops on a wire turn to ice?

Last night, lying in bed,
I remembered how, pensioners both,
before sleep, winter come,
your warm foot suddenly
would console my cold one.

(iii) Swan Song

Night fairground music
and, like kids, we sat astride
daft horses bouncing on
the lit-wide Merry-Go-Round
to swagger away, serene,
old lovers hand in hand.

Now, solemn, I watch
the spellbound moon again,
its unfocused clone drowned
in Hampstead's rush-dark pond
where a lone swan sings
without a sound.

POSTSCRIPT

January 7th 2007

Too often now, half somnolent, I would go
like Yeats to a fortunate Lake Isle where
unblemished water-lilies never die
and no solitary swan floats by
from everlasting to everlasting.

And in the tranquil orchard of this Isle
I'd plunder such paradisal apples
that Cezanne could have painted – apples
no bird would have dared to peck at,
fraudulent but beautiful.

Yes, I would go there rapt, recreant,
and stay there because, sweet, you're not here
till, self-scolded, I would recollect
my scruffy odorous Uncle Isidore
(surely one of the elect) who played

unsettling, attenuated music
long after a string had snapped,
whose beard bent down to interject,
'Little boy, who needs all the lyric strings?
Is the great world perfect?'

Appendices

APPENDIX ONE

The Young Man of The Ancient Race Who Was Carried Off by a Lion When Asleep in the Field

(Dictated in 1875 in the Katkop dialect (to Dr Bleek) by a bushman who had it from his mother)

A young man was the one who, formerly hunting, ascended a hill; he became sleepy; while he sat looking around for game he became sleepy. And he thought that he would first lie down; for he was not a little sleepy. For what could have happened to him today? because he had not previously felt like this.

And he lay down on account of it; and he slept, while a lion came; it went to the water, because the noonday heat had 'killed' it; it was thirsty; and it espied the man lying asleep; and it took up the man.

And the man awoke startled; and he saw that it was a lion which had taken him up. And he thought that he would not stir; for the lion would biting kill him, if he stirred; he would just see what the lion intended to do; for the lion appeared to think that he was dead.

And the lion carried him to a zwart-storm tree; and the lion laid him in it. And the lion thought that it would continue to be thirsty if it ate the man; it would first go to the water, that it might go to drink; it would come afterwards to eat, when it had drunk; for it would continue to be thirsty if it ate.

And it trod, pressing in the man's head between the stems of the zwart-storm tree; and it went back. And the man turned his head a little. And the lion looked back on account of it; namely, why had the man's head moved? when it had first thought that it had trodden, firmly fixing the man's head. And the lion thought that it did not seem to have laid the man nicely; for, the man fell over. And it again trod, pressing the man's head into the middle of the stems of zwart-storm tree. And it licked the man's eyes' tears. And the man wept; hence it licked the man's eyes. And the man felt that a stick did not a little pierce the hollow at the back of his head; and the man turned his head a little, while he looked steadfastly at the lion, he turned his head a little. And the lion looked to see why it was that the thing seemed as if the man had moved. And it licked the man's eyes' tears. And the lion thought it would tread, thoroughly pressing down the man's head, that it might really see whether it had been the one who had not laid the man down nicely. For, the thing seemed as if the man had stirred. And the man saw that the thing seemed as if the lion suspected that he was alive; and he did not stir, although the stick was piercing him. And the lion saw that the thing appeared as if it had laid the man down nicely; for the man did not stir; and it went a few steps away, and it looked towards the man, while the man drew

up his eyes; he looked through his eyelashes; he saw
what the lion was doing. And the lion went away,
ascending the hill; and the lion descended the hill on
the other side, while the man gently turned his head
because he wanted to see whether the lion had really
gone. And he saw that the lion appeared to have
descended the hill on the other side; and he perceived
that the lion again raising its head stood peeping
behind the top of the hill; because the lion thought
that the thing had seemed as if the man were alive;
therefore, it first wanted again to look thoroughly. For,
it seemed as if the man had intended to arise; for, it
had thought that the man had been feigning death.
And it saw that the man was still lying down; and it
thought that it would quickly run to the water, that
it might go to drink, that it might again quickly come
out from the water, that it might come to eat. For, it
was hungry; it was one who was not a little thirsty;
therefore, it just intended to go to drink, that it might
come afterwards to eat, when it had drunk.

The man lay looking at it, at that which it did; and
the man saw that its head's turning away and disap-
pearing with which it turned away and disappeared,
seemed as if it had altogether gone. And the man
thought that he would first lie still, that he might see
whether the lion would not again come peeping. For,
it is a thing which is cunning; it would intend to deceive
him, that the thing might seem as if it had really gone
away; while it thought that he would arise; for he had
seemed as if he stirred. For, it did not know why the

man had, when it thought that it had laid the man down nicely, the man had been falling over. Therefore, it thought that it would quickly run, that it might quickly come, that it might come to look whether the man still lay. And the man saw that a long time had passed since it again came to peep at him; and the thing seemed as if it had altogether gone. And the man thought that he would first wait a little; for, he would otherwise startle the lion, if the lion were still at this place. And the man saw that a little time had now passed, and he had not perceived the lion; and the thing seemed as if it had really gone away.

And he did nicely at the place yonder where he lay; he did not arise and go; for, he arose, he first sprang to a different place, while he wished that the lion should not know the place to which he seemed to have gone. He, when he had done in this manner, ran in a zigzag direction, while he desired that the lion should not smell out his footsteps, that the lion should not know the place to which he seemed to have gone; that the lion, when it came, should come to seek about for him there. Therefore, he thought that he would run in a zigzag direction, so that the lion might not smell out his footsteps; that he might go home; for, the lion, when it came, would come to seek for him. Therefore, he would not run straight into the house; for the lion, when it came and missed him, would intend to find his footprints, that the lion might, following his spoor, seek for him, that the lion might see whether it could not get hold of him.

Therefore, when he came out at the top of the hill, he called out to the people at home about it, that he had just been 'lifted up'; while the sun stood high, he had been 'lifted up' therefore, they must look out many hartebeest-skins, that they might roll him up in them; for he had just been 'lifted up', while the sun was high. Therefore, he thought that the lion would — when it came out from the place to which it had gone — it would come and miss him; it would resolve to seek and track him out. Therefore, he wanted the people to roll him up in many hartebeest-skins, so that the lion should not come and get him. For, they were those who knew that the lion is a thing which acts thus to the thing which it has killed, it does not leave it, when it has not eaten it. Therefore, the people must do this with the hartebeest-skins, the people must roll him up in them; and also in mats; these are things which the people must roll him up in, in order that the lion should not get him.

And the people did so; the people rolled him in mats, and also in hartebeest-skins, which they rolled together with the mats. For, the man was the one who had spoken thus to them about it; therefore it was that they rolled him up in hartebeest-skins, while they felt that their hearts' young man he was whom they did not wish the lion to eat. Therefore, they intended to hide him well, that the lion should not get hold of him. For, a young man whom they did not a little love he was. Therefore, they did not wish the lion to eat him; and they said that they would cover the young man with the hut's sheltering bushes so that the lion, when it came, should come seeking about for the young man; it should not get hold of the young man, when it came; it should come seeking about for him.

And the people went out to seek for kuisse (an edible root); and they dug out kuisse; and they brought home kuisse, at noon, and they baked kuisse. And an old Bushman, as he went along getting wood for his wife, in order that his wife might make a fire above the kuisse, espied the lion, as the lion came over the top of the hill, at the place which the young man had come over. And he told the house folk about it; and he spoke, he said: 'Ye are those who see the hill yonder, its top, the place yonder where that young man came over, what it looks like!'

And the young man's mother spoke, she said: 'Ye must not allow the lion to come into the huts; ye must shoot it dead, when it has not yet come to the huts.'

And the people slung on their quivers; and they went to meet the lion; and they were shooting at the lion; the lion would not die, although the people were shooting at it.

And another old woman spoke, she said: 'Ye must give to the lion a child, in order that the lion may go away from us.' The lion answered, it said that it did not want a child; for, it wanted the person whose eyes' tears it had licked; he was the one whom it wanted.

And the other people speaking, said: 'In what manner were ye shooting at the lion that ye could not manage to kill the lion?' And another old man spoke, he said:

'Can ye not see that it must be a sorcerer? It will not die when we are shooting at it; for, it insists upon having the man whom it carried off.'

The people threw children to the lion; the lion did not want the children which the people threw to it; for, it, looking, left them alone.

The people were shooting at it, while it sought for the man — that it might get hold of the man — the people were shooting at it. The people said: 'Ye must bring for us assegais, we must kill the lion.' The people were shooting at it; it did not seem as if the people were shooting at it; they were stabbing it with assegais, while they intended to stab it to death. It did not seem as if the people were stabbing it; for, it continued to seek for the young man; it said it wanted the young man whose tears it had licked; he was the one whom it wanted.

It scratched asunder, breaking to pieces for the people the huts, while it scratched asunder, seeking for the young man. And the people speaking, said: 'Can ye not see that the lion will not eat the children whom we have given to it?' And the people speaking, said: 'Can ye not see that a sorcerer it must be?' And the people speaking, said, 'Ye must give a girl to the lion, that we may see whether the lion will not eat her, that it may go away.' The lion did not want the girl; for, the lion only wanted the man whom it had carried off; he was the one whom it wanted.

And the people spoke, they said, they did not know in what manner they should act towards the lion, for, it had been morning when they shot at the lion; the lion would not die; for, it had when the people were shooting at it, it had been walking about. 'Therefore, we do not know in what manner we shall act towards the lion. For the children whom we gave to the lion, the lion has refused, on account of the man whom it had carried off.'

And the people speaking, said: 'Say ye to the young man's mother about it, that she must, although she loves the young man, she must take out the young man, she must give the young man to the lion, even if he be the child of her heart. For, she is the one who sees that the sun is about to set, while the lion is threatening us; the lion will not go and leave us; for, it insists upon having the young man.'

And the young man's mother spoke, she said: 'Ye may give my child to the lion; ye shall not allow the lion to eat my child; that the lion may go walking about; for, ye shall killing lay it upon my child; that it may die, like my child; that it may die, lying upon my child.'

And the people, when the young man's mother had thus spoken, the people took the young man out from the hartebeest-skins in which they had rolled him up, they gave the young man to the lion. And the lion bit the young man to death; the people when it was biting at the young man, were shooting at it; the people were stabbing it; and it bit the young man to death.

And the lion spoke, it said to the people about it,

that this time was the one at which it would die; for, it had got hold of the man for whom it had been seeking; it had got hold of him!

And it died, while the man also lay dead; it also lay dead, with the man.

Henry King

Exequy on his Wife

Accept, thou shrine of my dead saint,
Instead of dirges, this complaint;
And, for sweet flowers to crown thy
    hearse,
Receive a strew of weeping verse
From thy grieved friend whom thou
    might'st see
Quite melted into tears for thee.
    Dear loss! since thy untimely fate,
My task hath been to meditate
On thee, on thee! Thou art the book,
The library whereon I look,
Though almost blind. For thee, loved
    clay,
I languish on, not live, the day . . .
Thou hast benighted me; thy set
This eve of blackness did beget,
Who wast my day (though overcast
Before thou hadst thy noontide past).
And I remember must in tears
Thou scarce hadst seen so many years

As day tells hours. By thy clear sun
My love and fortune first did run;
But thou wilt never more appear
Folded within my hemisphere,
Since both thy light and motion,
Like a fled star, is fallen and gone,
And 'twixt me and my soul's dear wish
The earth now interposed is . . .
 I could allow thee for a time
To darken me and my sad clime;
Were it a month, a year, or ten,
I would thine exile live till then,
And all that space my mirth adjourn,
So thou would'st promise to return,
And putting off thy ashy shroud
At length disperse this sorrow's cloud.
But woe is me! the longest date
Too narrow is to calculate
These empty hopes; never shall I
Be so much blest as to descry
A glimpse of thee, till that day come
Which shall the earth to cinders doom,
And a fierce fever must calcine
The body of this world — like thine,
My little world! That fit of fire
Once off, our bodies shall aspire
To our souls' bliss; then we shall rise
And view ourselves with clearer eyes
In that calm region where no night
Can hide us from each other's sight.
 Meantime thou hast her, earth! much good
May my harm do thee; since it stood

With Heaven's will I might not call
Her longer mine, I give thee all
My short-lived right and interest
In her whom living I loved best.
Be kind to her, and prithee look
Thou write into thy Doomsday book
Each parcel of this rarity
Which in thy casket shrined doth lie,
As thou wilt answer Him that lent —
Not gave — thee my dear monument.
So close the ground, and 'bout her shade
Black curtains draw; my bride is laid.
Sleep on, my Love, in thy cold bed
Never to be disquieted!
My last goodnight! Thou wilt not wake
Till I thy fate shall overtake:
Till age, or grief, or sickness must
Marry my body to that dust
It so much loves, and fill the room
My heart keeps empty in thy tomb.
Stay for me there! I will not fail
To meet thee in that hollow vale.
And think not much of my delay —
I am already on the way,
And follow thee with all the speed
Desire can make, or sorrow breed.
Each minute is a short degree
And every hour a step towards thee.
    'Tis true — with shame and grief I yield —
Thou, like the van, first took'st the field;
And gotten hast the victory
In thus adventuring to die

Before me, whose more years might crave
A just precedence in the grave.
But hark! my pulse, like a soft drum,
Beats my approach, tells thee I come;
And slow howe'er my marches be,
I shall at last sit down by thee.
The thought of this bids me go on
And wait my dissolution
With hope and comfort. Dear, forgive
The crime — I am content to live
Divided, with but half a heart,
Till we shall meet and never part.

APPENDIX THREE

From: *Doodles from my Workbook*

What is revenge but a dead bird being eaten by a worm?

When a tall person meets a short one, the latter stands up straight.

Hilarity is not welcome at the breakfast table.

The longer a politician remains in power the better he can say what he means without meaning what he says.

Fame wears jewels over her sores.

An original is temporarily cheapened by its copy.

To bury the hatchet is unfortunately a unilateral act.

Every charismatic man is not only unpredictable but has a woman within him trying to get out.

Gratitude is a temporary phenomenon.

Those two tall trees you saw leaning towards each other whose furthest branches interlocked, the wind busy with their leaves, were discussing in whispers The Pathetic Fallacy.

Envy holds a dagger.

We are never bored when we are in the company of an enemy.

If you are happy do not ask yourself too many questions.

Lovers in bed are all guilty of word abuse.

Of two men the man from Porlock is always the one who is cheerful.

The final letter Z has its back to the abyss. Listen, it's on its knees praying.

Elias Canetti

The Orchestral Conductor
From: *Crowds and Power*

There is no more obvious expression of power than the performance of a conductor. Every detail of his public behaviour throws light on the nature of power. Someone who knew nothing about power could discover all its attributes, one after another, by careful observation of a conductor. The reason why this has never been done is obvious: the music the conductor evokes is thought to be the only thing that counts; people take it for granted that they go to concerts to hear symphonies and no one is more convinced of this than the conductor himself. He believes that his business is to serve music and to interpret it faithfully.

A conductor ranks himself first among the servants of music. He is so full of it that the idea of his activity having another, non-musical meaning never enters his head. No one would be more astonished than he at the following interpretation of it.

The conductor *stands*: ancient memories of what it

meant when man first stood upright still play an important part in any representations of power. Then, he is the only person who stands. In front of him sits the orchestra and behind him the audience. He stands on a dais and can be seen both from in front and from behind. In front his movements act on the orchestra and behind on the audience. In giving his actual directions he uses only his hands, or his hands and a baton. Quite small movements are all he needs to wake this or that instrument to life or to silence it at will. He has the power of life and death over the voices of the instruments; one long silent will speak again at his command. Their diversity stands for the diversity of mankind; an orchestra is like an assemblage of different types of men. The willingness of its members to obey him makes it possible for the conductor to transform them into a unit, which he then embodies.

The complexity of the work he performs means that he must be alert. Presence of mind is among his essential attributes; law-breakers must be curbed instantly. The code of laws, in the form of the score, is in his hands. There are others who have it too and can check the way it is carried out, but the conductor alone decides what the law is and summarily punishes any breach of it. That all this happens in public and is visible in every detail gives the conductor a special kind of self-assurance. He grows accustomed to being seen and becomes less and less able to do without it.

The immobility of the audience is as much part of

the conductor's design as the obedience of the orchestra.
They are under a compulsion to keep still. Until he
appears they move about and talk freely among themselves. The presence of the players disturbs no one;
indeed they are scarcely noticed. Then the conductor
appears and everyone becomes still. He mounts the
rostrum, clears his throat and raises his baton; silence
falls. While he is conducting no one may move and as
soon as he finishes they must applaud. All their desire
for movement, stimulated and heightened by the music,
must be banked up until the end of the work and must
then break loose. The conductor bows to the clapping
hands; for them he returns to the rostrum again and
again, as often as they want him to. To them, and to
them alone, he surrenders; it is for them that he really
lives. The applause he receives is the ancient salute to
the victor, and the magnitude of his victory is measured by its volume. Victory and defeat become the frame-
work within which his spiritual economy is ordered.
Apart from these nothing counts; everything that the
lives of other men contain is for him transformed into
victory or defeat.

During a concert, and for the people gathered
together in the hall, the conductor is a leader. He stands
at their head with his back to them. It is him they
follow, for it is he who goes first. But, instead of his
feet, it is his hands which lead them. The movement
of the music, which his hands bring about, represents
the path his feet would be the first to tread. The crowd
in the hall is carried forward by him. During the whole

performance of a work they never see his face. He is merciless; there are no intervals for rest. They see his back always in front of them, as though it were their goal. If he turned round even once the spell would be broken. The road they were travelling would suddenly cease to exist and there would be nothing but a hall full of disillusioned people without movement or impetus. But the conductor can be relied on not to turn round, for, while the audience follows him behind, in front he is faced by a small army of professional players, which he must control. For this purpose, too, he uses his hands, but here they not only point the way, as they do for those behind him, but they also give orders.

His eyes hold the whole orchestra. Every player feels that the conductor sees him personally, and, still more, hears him. The voices of the instruments are opinions and convictions on which he keeps a close watch. He is omniscient, for, while the players have only their own parts in front of them, he has the whole score in his head, or on his desk. At any given moment he knows precisely what each player should be doing. His attention is everywhere at once, and it is to this that he owes a large part of his authority. He is inside the mind of every player. He knows not only what each *should* be doing, but also what he *is* doing. He is the living embodiment of law, both positive and negative. His hands decree and prohibit. His ears search out profanation.

Thus for the orchestra the conductor literally

embodies the work they are playing, the simultaneity of the sounds as well as their sequence; and since, during the performance, nothing is supposed to exist except this work, for so long is the conductor the ruler of the world.

Translated by Carol Stewart

APPENDIX FIVE

Sigmund Freud's Letter to Sandor Ferenczi Written on December 13th, 1931

I see that the differences between us come to a head in a technical detail which is well worth discussing. You have not made a secret of the fact that you kiss your patients and let them kiss you; I had also heard that from a patient of my own. Now when you decide to give a full account of your technique and its results you will have to choose between two ways: either you relate this or you conceal it. The latter, as you may well think, is dishonourable. What one does in one's technique one has to defend openly. Besides, both ways soon come together. Even if you don't say so yourself it will soon get known just as I knew it before you told me.

Now I am assuredly not one of those who from prudishness or from consideration of bourgeois convention would condemn little erotic gratifications of this kind. And I am also aware that in the time of the Nibelungs a kiss was a harmless greeting granted to every guest. I am further of the opinion that analysis is possible even in Soviet Russia where so far as the State is concerned there is full sexual freedom. But that does not alter the facts that we are not living in Russia and that with us a kiss signifies a certain erotic intimacy. We have hitherto in our technique held to the conclusion that patients are to be refused erotic gratifications. You know too that where more extensive gratifications are not to be had milder caresses very easily take over their role, in love affairs, on the stage, etc.

Now picture what will be the result of publishing your technique. There is no revolutionary who is not driven out of the field by a still more radical one. A number of independent thinkers in matters of technique will say to themselves: why stop at a kiss? Certainly one gets further when one adopts 'pawing' as well, which after all doesn't make a baby. And then bolder ones will come along who will go further to peeping and showing – and soon we shall have accepted in the technique of analysis the whole repertoire of demiviergerie and petting-parties, resulting in an enormous increase of patients in psychoanalysis among both analysts and patients. The new adherent, however, will easily claim too much of this interest for himself, the younger of our colleagues will find it hard to stop at the point they originally intended, and God the Father, Ferenczi, gazing at the lively scene he has created will perhaps say to himself: maybe after all I should have halted in my technique of motherly affection *before* the kiss . . .

Ludwig van Beethoven
from The Heiligenstadt Testament

. . . Yet only consider that for six years I have been suffering an incurable affliction, aggravated by imprudent physicians. Year after year deceived by the hope of an improvement, finally forced to contemplate the prospect of a lasting illness, whose cure may take years or may even be impossible, born with a fiery, impulsive temperament, sensible, even, to the distractions of social life, I was yet compelled early in my life to isolate myself, to spend my life in solitude. Even if at times I wished to overcome all this, oh, how harshly I was driven back by the doubly grievous experience of my bad hearing, and yet I could not prevail upon myself to say to men: speak louder, shout, for I am deaf. Oh, how could I possibly admit to being defective in the very sense which should have been more highly developed in me than in other men, a sense which once I possessed in its most perfect form, a form as perfect as few in my profession, surely, know or have known in the past. Oh, I cannot do it. Therefore you must forgive me if you should see me draw back when I would gladly mingle with you. My affliction is all the more painful to me because it leads to such misinterpretations of my conduct. Recreation in human society, refined conversation, mutual effusions of thought are denied to me. Almost quite alone, I may commit myself to social life only as far as the most urgent needs demand. I must live like an exile. When I do venture near some social gathering, I am seized with a burning terror, the fear that I may be placed in the dangerous position of having to reveal my condition. So, too, it has been with me during the past half-year, which I spent in the country. When my reasonable physician ordered me to spare my hearing as much as possible, he almost accorded with my natural disposition, although sometimes, overpowered by the urge to seek society, I disobeyed his orders. But what an humiliation when someone standing next to me heard a flute in the distance and I heard nothing, or when someone heard the shepherd sing and, again, I heard nothing. Such occurrences brought me to the verge of despair. I might easily have put an end to my life. Only one thing, Art, held me back. . . .

Heiligenstadt, October 1802

Translated by Michael Hamburger

ACKNOWLEDGEMENTS

Alex Comfort: 'Notes for my Son' from *The Dove in Flames* ed. Norman Kreitman. Reproduced by permission © The Estate of Alex Comfort

Boris Pasternak: 'It is not seemly' translated by Lydia Pasternak Slater from *Fifty Poems* (Unwin Books). Reproduced by permission © The Estate of Lydia Pasternak

Ted Hughes: 'How Water Began to Play' from *Collected Poems* (Faber). Reproduced by permission

Sidney Keyes: 'Hopes for a Lover' from *Collected Poems* (Carcanet). Reproduced by permission

David Wright: 'A Funeral Oration' from *To the Gods the Shades* (Carcanet). Reproduced by permission

Kit Wright: 'Everyday in Every Way' from *Poems 1974–1983* (Hutchinson). Reproduced by permission

R. S. Thomas: 'A Marriage' from *Collected Later Poems 1988–2000* (Bloodaxe Books, 2004)

James Reeves: 'Old Crabbed Men' from *The Password* (William Heinemann). Reproduced by permission © The Estate of James Reeves

Ludwig Beethoven: *Beethoven's Letters, Journals, Conversations* edited, translated and introduced by Michael Hamburger, © 1984. Reprinted by kind permission of Thames & Hudson Ltd, London

Elias Canetti: 'The Orchestral Conductor' from *Crowds and Power* (Gollancz). Published by Weidenfeld and Nicolson, a division of The Orion Publishing Group. Reproduced by permission

Arthur Jacobs: 'Travelling Abroad' from *Collected Poems* (Menard Press/Hearing Eye). Reproduced by permission

Dabney Stuart: 'Sunburst' from *Modern Poets in Focus 3* ed. D. Abse. (Corgi)

'Sometimes' from *Selected Poems* (Seren). Reproduced by permission

C. P. Cafavy: 'A Prince from Western Libya' translated by E. Keeley and P. Sherrard from *Collected Poems* (Chatto & Windus). Reproduced by permission of The Random House Group Ltd and Rogers, Coleridge & White Ltd

Laurie Lee: 'Day of these Days' from *The Pocket Poets* (Vista Books). Reproduced by permission of PFD on behalf of The Estate of Laurie Lee © 1960

Peter Viereck: 'Of Course Not' from *Strike through the Mask* (Scribner). Reproduced by permission © The Estate of Peter Viereck

Dannie Abse: 'The Malham Bird', 'With Compliments', 'Postcard to His Wife', and 'Lachrymae' from *Running Late* (Hutchinson). All his other poems from *New and Collected Poems* (Hutchinson) except for the new unpublished 'Postcard to His Wife' and the recent 'January 7th Postscript'

Every effort has been made to contact all copyright holders. The publishers will be glad to make good in future editions any errors or omissions brought to their attention.

www.poetryarchive.org

Remembering Joan Abse:
www.joanabse.pwp.blueyonder.co.uk